The
Ogham
Stone

The
Ogham
Stone

an anthology of
contemporary
Ireland

edited by
Gerald Dawe and
Michael Mulreany

IPA

INSTITUTE OF PUBLIC
ADMINISTRATION

First published 2001
Institute of Public Administration
57–61 Lansdowne Road
Dublin 4
Ireland

ISBN 1 902448 53 7 hbk
     1 902448 59 6 pbk

British Library cataloguing-in-publication data
A catalogue record for this book is available from the British Library

Ogham Stone drawing by Peter Knuttel
Designed by Butler Claffey Design, Dún Laoghaire
Typeset in 10/11.5 Garamond by Computertype Ltd., Dublin
Printed by Criterion Press, Dublin, Ireland

To the memory of
Michael Hartnett

Contents

 **Brian Farrell**

Introduction

Saul Bellow once wrote, no doubt provocatively, that people in power have little esteem for writers because there was little evidence from modern literature that authors were thinking about significant questions.

This may be true in many modern societies, but I doubt that it is true in Ireland. Various features of Irish writing — the enjoyment and deployment of words, sense of place, love of character, use of personification, awareness of the continuity of history and critical probing of the diverse strands of national identity — reflect the fabric of our society and create a general respect for literature.

Of course there are differences of opinion about our literary heritage and development. There is lively debate about cultural commodification and stimulating argument about the evolution of the official stance on literature from the dark days of censorship to the current portrayal of writers on bank notes. But, overall, it seems to me that there is a significant level of official recognition and public esteem for both our literary canon and contemporary writers. This is not simply an acknowledgement of the contribution of literary awards and achievements to the enhancement of the country's international reputation, it is also a recognition of how literature helps create, preserve and advance our cultural identity and how it has interrogated social, political and economic development since the foundation of the state.

It is fitting, therefore, that the Institute of Public Administration, Ireland's public service development agency, acknowledges the importance of literature to an understanding of Irish life and the unfolding story of modern Ireland. This began formally, twenty years ago, when the Institute first offered literature courses as an integral part of programmes for US students coming to Ireland to study politics and work as interns in the Houses of the Oireachtas. It is a testimony to the growth of these programmes that generous subventions from the Catholic University of America, Northeastern University and Suffolk University, Boston have supported the production of this book.

Over the intervening years an extraordinary and talented array of writers have been associated with programmes at the Institute and it is essentially these writers who are anthologised in this book. They represent diverse aspects of Irish writing — poetry, fiction and the essay — across different generations and traditions, and illustrate the vibrancy and creativity of con- temporary Irish writing.

Why *The Ogham Stone?* Ogham, the oldest form of Irish

script, was a system of representing letters by groups of short lines varying in position, length and number. It was too cumbersome to survive: if this book was written in ogham script it would stretch to well over a kilometre! However, the ogham stone, the type of standing stone inscribed with ogham script, has survived and indeed transcended its time to assume a contemporary meaning as a symbol of Irish literature and learning. It is a symbol that recalls Yeats's dramatic line, written near the end of his life: 'And ancient Ireland knew it all'.

Educators rightly acknowledge the power of this symbol: students and visitors to the IPA at Lansdowne Road have for decades been greeted by an ogham stone, a twentieth-century re-statement of an image almost fifteen centuries old. It was relatively easy, therefore, to choose a title for the book.

This publication is an appropriate occasion to thank many people who have participated in and contributed to the parliamentary internship programme, including members of the Oireachtas who sponsored the students, the Academic Council which oversaw their scholarly performance, the IPA staff who guided their daily rounds, Bob Cormack at Queen's University and, of course, the students themselves. Warm thanks are due to the office staff at Leinster House, the ushers and the Superintendent of the Houses of the Oireachtas, Commandant Eamon O'Donohoe, for his constant support and co-operation.

The production of *The Ogham Stone* has demanded time, patience and energy. The contributors have been generous in allocating their work and time, and patient in dealing with the inevitable queries. At the IPA, Jennifer Armstrong and Denis O'Brien were most helpful at various stages of the drafting and design. But, one debt of gratitude surpasses all others: combining tireless effort with self-effacing style, Patricia Ryan, at successive stages, made the difference between order and chaos; to her is due a special word of thanks.

Sadly, during the preparation of *The Ogham Stone*, one of the authors, Michael Hartnett, died. The book commences with a previously unpublished poem that he had promised the editors. He was kind-hearted, courteous and, of course, cultured, and it is to his memory that the book is dedicated.

Michael Hartnett

Something Secret

do Neasa

. . . something secret about flowers
as if they'd witnessed dramas in the past
(captive in a vase, inquisitive,
with eyes like God),
as if they'd felt when hurt souls clashed.

Some (like the urgent women seen at Mass
whose hands seem cut from wax,
jet-black beads about their wrists)
have petals (where Christ's blood was splashed)
that fix upon the sun, as women on one saint
fix eyes and see but one beloved face.

Even in the dark their perfume prays.

Nuala Ní Dhomhnaill

(translation: **Aodán Mac Póilin**)

Teacht an Dé

Sileann an fhoinse bheannaithe i gclós na mainistreach.
Scinneann an sciathán leathair tríd an aer.
Ólaimíd rogha gach dí is raidhse fíona.
Stopann lámh an naoimh orainn na saigheada.

Ar fhaobhar mo radhairce, ar fhaobhar samhlaíochta
braithim an paintéar breac ag teacht inár ngaobhar.
Siúlann sé isteach sa tseomra ar lapaí tostmhara
is ólann sé a sháith den bhfíon. Tá faobhar

na bhfiacal fós faoi cheilt aige go daingean.
Tá na liodáin coinnithe go ciúin i dtruaill.
Luascann a eireaball idir scáil is loinnir,
ag tonnaíocht gan mhairg idir beatha is bás.

Is a Dhé a thaibhsíonn leis i gcló an tairbh
nó mar nathaIr mhór ag tionlac' slua na marbh,
níl agam réidh faoi do dhéin mar íobairt dhóite
ach m'anam féin, ar tinneall ar bhruach na póite.

The Coming of the God

In the monastery yard the holy fountain trickles.
A bat darts through the air.
We drink the best of liquor and lashings of wine.
The saint's hand shields us from the arrows.

At the edge of my vision, imagination's edge,
I sense the stippled panther drawing near.
He steals into the room on noiseless paws
and drinks his fill of wine. His bladed

teeth still firmly out of sight,
the prayers for the dying ready but unread.
His indifferent tail switches from dark to light,
pulsing from death to life, from life to death.

O God who appears in the form of a bull
or a serpent escorting the host of the dead,
the only burnt offering I have to sacrifice
is my own fidgeting, nearly blind-drunk, soul.

Melusine

Is léi i gcónaí
an tigh ina mairim
is gach a bhfuil ann:
caisleán uaigneach cois locha
is dabhach mór folctha
i lár mo sheomra leapan

Caitheann sí an lá go léir ann
gach aon Dé Sathairn, ar a sáimhín
só, ar a cúilín seamhrach,
ag meidhréis is ag gleáchas
san uisce alabhog, ag tomadh ann
is á scaoileadh thairsti anall.

'Má tá iomard nó máchail
ar gach uile dhuine clainne agam
bíodh sé amhlaidh. Is cuma liom.
Ní mór liom díobh iad
ach is mór an t-iontas liom
iad a bheith ann in aon chor.'

Is fíor di. Ba mhaith an mhaise dhúinn
nár cheistíomair í níos crua.
B'fholláin dúinn nár bhuail an smaoineamh sinn
silence ar bith a bhualadh uirthi
is sinn ar thóir na fírinne.

Laistiar den gceist
tá fiosracht. Laistiar den bhfios
tá éitheach. Laistíos den urlár
tá na mairbh
ag osnaíl is ag éagaoin.

Is cá bhfios dúinn cad a dh'imigh orthu?
Nó cá bhfios dúinn cad a d'éiligh?
Nó cá bhfios dúinn an gníomh gaile groí
a thionscnaigh sí chun éaló?

Melusine

She still owns
the house I live in
and all in it:
a lonely lakeside castle
and a great bathtub
in the middle of my bedroom.

She spends all day there
every Saturday, happy
as Larry, lolling at her ease,
frisking and playing
in the lukewarm water, dunking under
and splashing around.

'If every single child of mine
is afflicted or maimed
so be it. I don't care.
Hell slap it into them,
but I'm greatly surprised
that they're here at all.'

She's right. It's well for us
we did not question her more closely.
It's well for us we did not think
to force her into silence
while we searched for the truth.

Behind the question
the need to know. Behind the knowledge
a lie. Beneath the floor
the dead
sigh and groan.

And how do we know what happened to them?
Or how do we know what was demanded?
Or how do we know by what heroic deed
she contrived to escape?

La Ginestra

i. m. Theo Ryan

Maireann tú fós.
Mar a phéacann an giolcach sléibhe
nó an scuab chumhra ar shleasaibh loma
an bholcáin Vesuvius.

Thíos faoi, ar lár faoi bhrat dlúth luaithe
luíonn na cathracha ársa, Pompeii
is Herculaneum, iad dearmhadta
is titithe i ndíchuimhne dhoimhin na ndaoine.

Tá an deannach tiubh ina luí
ar gach teampall is gach amharclann,
gach foirgneamh ard poiblí.
Na tithe folcaidh, spóirt is fothragaithe

ina bhfásaigh ghoirte mar aon leis na tithe tábhairne.
Gach uile *villa* fairsing is príobháideach
gona fhallaí freisceó is a chuid urlár mósáice
múchta faoi thaiséadach túfa

is gan a thuairisc le fáil níos mó.
Thit an sliabh orthu mar a thitfeadh
úll sa bhfómhar anuas ar nead seangán
ag réabhadh is ag cloí

a n-oibreacha poiblí; an t-ollmhaitheas
curtha le chéile go tíosach, cnúisciúnta
le tréaniarracht
ag a mhuintir neamhdhíomhaoin.

(Ár gcomaoin sin ort, a fharraige mhór
is sinn ag mún le gaoith.
Is mór an ní an neart, a dúirt an dreoilín
is é ag caitheamh na péiste le haill.)

Mar sin a imíonn ár n-oibreacha is ár bpoimpeanna
in ainm phoillíní an diabhail
is nára maith againn. Titeann
impireachtaí is sibhialtachtaí ar lár.

La Ginestra

i. m. Theo Ryan

You still live.
As the mountain reed or the fragrant broom
sprout on the naked volcanic
slopes of Vesuvius.

Below, under a drift of packed ash
lie the ancient cities, Pompeii
and Herculaneum, forgotten
in the deep misrememberance of mankind.

The thick dust lies
on every temple and every theatre,
every tall public building.
The bathhouses and sports halls

are salt deserts as are the taverns.
Every single spacious private villa
with its frescoed walls and mosaic floors
is smothered under a shroud of tufa

its record no longer to be found.
The mountain fell upon them as an apple
would fall on an ants' nest
tearing and destroying

their public works; that commonweal
that was put together frugally, thriftily, carefully
by the great efforts
of its busy inhabitants.

(Here's an offering, great sea
as we piss with the wind.
Strength is wonderful, said the wren
tossing the worm over the cliff.)

This is how our works and pomps
go to the devil.
Bad luck to us. Empires
and civilizations fall.

Ach maireann tú fós
i gcuimhne an uile dhuine
a theangmhaigh riamh leat
nó a tháinig faoi réir do gháire

a d'aithin do spiorad neamhspléach
is do dhea-mhéin
atá chomh tréithiúil is comh buan
le bláth na scuaibe cumhra, nó an giolcach sléibhe

a fhásann at thaobh Vesuvius
riamh is i gcónaí
in ainneoin gach tubaiste a bhuaileann
mac an duine.

But you still live
in the memory of everyone
who ever met you
or came under the dominion of your smile,

who recognised your independent spirit
your good nature
that is as powerful and as enduring
as the blossom of the fragrant broom or the mountain reed

that grows on the slopes of Vesuvius
always and ever
in spite of every disaster that strikes
the sons of men.

Nóiméad Zen um Thráthnóna

Níl drithle fiú as an gcrann eoclaipe
gur gnách léi bheith ag luascadh sa ghaoth.
Is seiceadúir buan í ag claí bun an ghairdín
ag tabhairt fianaise ar gach puth a bhíonn san aer.

Tá gach driseog siochta mar a bheadh sí ar garda.
Tá na scamaill ina seasamh sa spéir.
Tá gach úll crochta go síoraí mar a bhí ar chrann Parthais
is an nathair fós gan teacht ar an saol.

Tá éinín ag canadh do mhanach na cille.
Tá Oisín ag marcaíocht ar chúlaibh mná na gruaige finne.
Tá an Daghdha ag luí le bandia na Bóinne.
Tá banríon na n-iasc ag caint le Urashima Taro.

Ansan corraíonn duilleog
is éiríonn crothóg liath ar leathmhaig eitilte.
Tá a gnáthráiméis ar siúl arís ag an meaig mhór
a bhíonn ag bodhradh mo chinn go coitianta ó dhíon thigh na
        comharsan.

Osclaíonn doras cóngarach dom, is tagann bleaist phopcheoil
faoim' dhéin; anois tá meaisín glórach ag lomadh faiche.
Searaim mé fhéin, go leathscéalach, as domhan an mhistéir
ag iarraidh breith ar eireabaillín giobalach mo thaibhrimh.

Zen in the Afternoon

Not so much as a glint from the eucalyptus tree
that used to sway with the wind,
a steadfast wind-gauge in the bottom garden hedge
witnessing every breath in the air.

Each briar is frozen as if on guard.
The clouds stand to attention in the sky.
Every apple hangs eternally as on the tree in Eden
before the serpent came into the world.

A bird sings to the forest anchorite.
Oisín rides behind the fair-haired woman.
The Daghda lies with the goddess of the Boyne.
The Fisher-queen speaks to Urashima Taro.

Then a leaf stirs
and a hooded crow lurches into flight.
The magpie on my neighbour's roof
deafens me once more with his usual gabble.

A door opens nearby, and a blast of pop music
fetches me back; a braying machine mows some lawn.
I shake myself, diffidently, from the world of mystery
trying to grasp the ragged tail of my reverie.

Éinín Bídeach

Léimeann éinín bídeach
ar chraobh uachtair an chrainn ghiúise
ar aghaidh na fuinneoige os mo chomhair.
Ní féidir liom a aithint
óna thoirt nó óna ghluaiseacht
an dreoilín é nó meantán
is tá léas na gréine am' dhalladh
ar a dhath.

Níl oiread na frí ann
ag luascadh ar an gcraobh uachtair.
Ní troimide é mo chroí
ag féachaint air i mbarr an chrainn ghiúise.

A Tiny Bird

A tiny bird starts
on the top branch of the fir tree
in front of the facing window.
I cannot tell
from its shape or its movement
if it is a wren or a tit
and the sun's back-light blinds me
to its colour.

It is no bigger than a gnat
as it sways on the upper branch.
Not heavier is my heart
seeing it in the top of the fir tree.

An Obair

An móta is bábhún Normannach a chonac isteach thar chuirtín
    crann
is mé ag tiomáint thar bráid go tapaidh ar an mbóthar,
áit éigin faoin dtuath in aice le Cill Mhaighneann
I gCo. na Mí, a thugann an ainm don áit. Sin í An Obair.

É sin is an cara mná is ansa liom ar domhan ag fáil bháis go mall
in Ospidéal an Adelaide: an grianghraf thíos im' phóca dúinn
    beirt inár mná óga
a tógadh lá Márta, an chéad lá earraigh i nGairdín na mBláth in
    Ankara
na Tuirce: sinn ag gáirí is gan tuairim againn ar cad a bhí
    romhainn:

aghaidh na mná Moslamaí ón Ailgéir a chonac le déanaí sa
    nuachtán
nuair a hinsíodh di go rabhthas tar éis an scornach a ghearradh
ar ochtar leanbh óg dá clann: an file iomráiteach Seirbeach
a bhí ina cheannaire ar mhórchampa géibhinn; an stairí litríochta
a chaith a chuid ama saor lena chairde ag imirt caide le plaosc
    dhaonna:

m'fhear céile a chaith sé lá i gcóma is mé ag féachaint amach
    fuinneoga
an tseomra feithimh ar an solas ag dorchú amuigh at an mbá
idir Dún Laoghaire is Beann Éadair, is ar theacht is imeacht na
    taoide:
trácht trom ar an mbóthar mar a raibh an saol Fódlach ag rith
    sall
is anall, ag plódú ar nós na nduilleog a bhí ag péacadh ar gach
    aon chrann:

— é seo go léir a thabhairt faoi ndeara is áit a dhéanamh dó id'
    chroí gan pléascadh,
é seo uile is an móta Normannach a chonac is mé ag gabháil na
    slí,
áit éigin faoin dtuath in aice le Cill Mhaighneann i gCo. na Mí —
An Obair. Sin í an obair. Sin í an obair nach éasca.

The Task

I saw a Norman motte and bailey through a curtain of trees
while speeding by on the road,
somewhere in the country near Kilmainham
in County Meath, which gives the place its name: Nobber.
So this is An Obair — 'the Works', 'the Task'.

That and my closest woman friend dying slowly
in the Adelaide Hospital: the photo in my pocket of both of us
        as young women,
taken on a March day, the first day of Spring in the Flower
        Garden in Ankara,
Turkey: laughing and ignorant of what the future held:

the face of the Algerian Muslim woman I saw recently in the
        paper
when she was told that the throats had been cut
of six of her young children: the eminent Serbian poet
who was commandant of a concentration camp; the literary
        historian
who relaxed with his friends playing football with a human head:

my husband who spent six days in a coma while I gazed out the
        window
of the waiting-room at the light darkening on the bay
between Dún Laoghaire and Howth, and at the tide coming and
        going:
heavy traffic on the road where everyone hurried hither
and thon, crowding together like the leaves which were thrusting
        on every tree:

— to see all this and make a place for it in your heart without
        bursting
all this and the Norman motte I saw in passing
somewhere in the country near Kilmainham in County Meath —
An Obair. The Task. The task which is not easy.

Tráigh Gheimhridh

Tá an tráigh folamh an dtaca seo 'bhliain,
chomh sciomartha scuabtha le leac tairseann,
sobal i dtaobh thuas di go líne barra taoide.
Is tíosach an bhean níocháin í an sáile.

Camóga, miongán capaill nó sliogán muirín
ní bhuaileann liom ar mo chamruathar
ach faid mo radhairc uaim amuigh ar an dtoinn
comhairím ocht gcinn de ghéanna giúrainn.

Snámhann siad go mómhar; an chuid eile dhínn
fanfaimíd tamall beag eile leis an mbiaiste,
le tráigheanna rabharta maisithe le trilseáin,
eireaball mhadraí rua, sceana mara agus sagairtíní.

A Winter Beach

The beach is empty at this time of year,
as scrubbed and scoured as a doorstep,
soapy foam right up to the tide-line.
The sea is a houseproud washerwoman.

On my walk I meet no hunchback scallops,
roaring buckies or clam shells
but far away among the waves
I count eight barnacle geese.

They swim serenely, the rest of us
must wait another while for the season of plenty,
plaited flood-tide beaches, spangled
with foxtails of dock-seeds, cowries, razor-pods.

Ceol

Maidin sa leaba, cé thógfadh orm é?
Nach bhfuil mo shaol go léir caite agam
ag tiomáint leanaí grabhsacha ar scoil.
Inniu an Satharn agus táid i bhfad uaim
is mar leithscéal breise is mar bharr iontais
tá sé ag cur sneachtaigh ar fuaid faid
agus leithead na hÉireann.

Brúim mo mhéar ar chnaipe agus tá R na G
ag tabhairt faisnéis na haimsire don lá inniu:
'Tá na bóithre ina ngloine, go háirithe san Oirthear.
Tá an mórbhóthar go Baile Átha Cliath ina reoleac
agus tá na mionbhóithre go léir faoi shneachta.
Beidh sé fuar agus gaofar.
Titfidh ráigeanna sneachtaigh ar fuaid na tíre
i rith an lae. Beidh na bóithre sleamhain
i scata áiteanna. Ní ardóidh an teocht
thar an reophointe. Tá fógra gála eisithe.'

Brúim arís is tá an BBC, Radio a trí,
ag líonadh an seomra le ceol ghealgháireach:
'Los Cantigas de Sancta Maria' ón Spáinn sa tríú céad déag.
Is léir an bhuntsraith Mhúrach leis na haeranna.
Tá ceol 'arabesque' an lae inniu féin
is seanmnaí fada na nArabach
le clos laistiar de, cé nach móide go dtaitneodh
smaoineamh dá leithéid leis an Rí Alfonsó a Deich
a thiomsaigh iad is ba chúis lena mbailiú.
Is cuma; fiú agus an seicteachas abú
maireann an ceol agus tugann sé leis an lá.

Éirím.
Tá an spéir chomh glan, an domhan chomh folamh.
An dúthaigh máguaird athraithe ó thalamh.
Braithim chomh dúr, im' phár ullamh
le scéal mo bheatha a rianú air.
Tá an ceol go hálainn.
Cloisim an ghrian ag éirí ann
is í ag rince fá thrí sa spéir
maidin fhuar reoite díreach mar í seo
seacht gcéad éigin bliain ó shin
sa Spáinn. Cuireann sé
dathana is foirmeacha ar foluain

Music

A morning in bed, who'd blame me?
Haven't I spent my whole life
driving crabbed kids to school.
Today is Saturday and they are far away
and as a further excuse, wonder of wonders,
snow is general
all over Ireland.

I press the button and R na G
is giving today's weather forecast:
'The roads are like glass, especially in the East.
The main road to Dublin is a sheet of ice
and all the minor roads are snowbound.
It will be cold and stormy.
Showers of snow will fall throughout the country
during the day. The roads will be treacherous
in some places. The temperature
will not rise above freezing. A gale warning has been issued.'

I press again and the BBC Third Programme
is filling the room with animated music:
'Los Cantigas de Sancta Maria' from thirteenth-century Spain.
The Moorish basis of the tunes is clear.
The 'arabesque' music of today
and the long Arabic melodic line
can be heard behind it, although it is unlikely
that such an idea would appeal to King Alfonso the Tenth
who compiled them and commissioned their collection.
No matter: though sectarianism is still alive and kicking
the music survives and wins the day.

I get up.
The sky is so clear, the world is so empty.
Everywhere around changed utterly.
I feel so dull, paper ready
to have the story of my life traced on it.
The music is wonderful.
I can hear in it the sun rising
and dancing three times in the sky
on a cold freezing day just like this
some seven hundred years ago
in Spain. It sends colours and shapes floating
in my mind

im' mheabhair
atá chomh bán le páipéar,
chomh glan, éadóchasach,
le baile fearainn tréigthe ón nDrochshaol
atá clúdaithe le sneachta.

which is as white as paper,
as clean, hopeless,
as an abandoned townland from Famine days
covered with snow.

Fíorláir na Filíochta

Tá capall ráis á cothú agam faoin staighre.
Fíorlair. An seachtú searrach baineann
ón seachtú searrach baineann. Tá gá aici
bheith seacht mbliana í stábla,
á cothú le fíoruisce is cruithneacht dhearg.

Ach i dtigh leathscoite ins na bruachbhailte
is deacair teacht ar stábla. Sin é an fáth
go bhfuil sí stobháilte agam isteach faoi chabha an staighre
an fhaid is a bhead ábalta bheith ina bun.

Sa lá bíonn sí discréideach.
Sa chapsholas ní dh'aithneofá í
thar ghnáth-thranglam an tí: cótaí báistí, buataisí,
an 'chaise longue' a bhíonn ag teastáil don lá gréine,
nó ceann des na heilimintí breise a bhíonn ag gabháilt leis an
     hoover.

Ach san oíche tugaim cead a cinn dí.
Cathim uaim an ceanrach is an béalbhach.
Scaoilim na giortaí, bainim di an diallait.
Ligim na srianta léi. Is léi an tigh go léir.

Labhrann sí thar n-ais liom.
Fágann sí teachtaireachtaí chomh hiontach
ar mheaisín freagartha an teileafóin
go mbím sceimhlithe im' bheathaidh á seinnt thar n-ais
uaireanta bíonn chomh fáidhiúil sin, chomh híogair.

Ach sé nádúr an ainmhí bheith achrannach.
Is minic a chuireann sí stailc suas
is diúltaíonn sí do m'ordaithe. Deineann sí cur isteach
ceart ar an ngréasán leictreamaighnéadach sa teach
le méid a cuid iarrachtaí ar bhriseadh amach.
Tá n'fheadar cé méid comhad caillte agam ar mo PhC
dá dheasca, is maidir leis an m*burglar alarm*
go sábhála Mac Dé sinn, ach bíonn sé ag imeacht go síoraí.
Samhlaigh duit féin an trioblóid a bhíonn agam
ag míniú an scéil don nGarda rothar gluaiste
a bhrostaíonn amach láithreach ar an bhfód,
chun a cheart féin a thabhairt dó. Mo leathscéalta giobalacha:
'Bhuel a gharda, is amhlaidh atá . . .'

Poetry's Thoroughbred Mare

I'm keeping a racehorse under the stairs.
A thoroughbred mare. The seventh female foal
of a seventh female foal. She needs
seven years stabling
fed on spring water and red wheat.

But in a suburban semi
it's hard to find a stable. That is why
I have stowed her in the glory-hole under the stairs
as long as I am able.

By day she is discreet.
In the twilight you wouldn't know her
from the usual household goods: raincoats, boots,
the 'chaise longue' that's needed for sunny days,
or one of the hoover's extra accoutrements.

But at night I give her her head,
throw off the halter and bridle,
loosen the girth, take off the saddle.
Let go the reins. The house is hers.

She talks back to me.
She leaves such strange messages
on the answering machine
that I am scared witless playing them back,
sometimes she is so prophetic, so sensitive.

But the beast's nature is to be perverse.
Sometimes she jibs
and refuses to do what she's told. She disrupts
the entire electromagnetic system in the house
with the force of her efforts to escape.
I don't know how many files I have lost on my PC
because of her, and as for the burglar alarm,
God save us, but it's always going off.
Imagine to yourself the trouble I have
explaining this to the motorbike cop
who rushes out immediately,
to give him his due. My ragged excuses:
'Well, Guard, it's like this . . .'

Is dála an bhuachalla
is an mactíre, ní foláir nó nach fada eile
a rithfidh liom. Ag dúnadh an dorais i ndiaidh an foghla.
Nó gníomh éigin eile díchéille ar an gcuma san.

Ach cén fáth go gcothaíonn tú í mar sin, cloisim tú ag rá.
Tá, gurb í mo dhóchas is m'aonábhar slánaithe í.
An chéad uair eile a bhuailfidh Tonn Tóime an duaircis
anuas sa mhullach aduaidh orm, go dtabharfaidh sí glan isteach
ar an míntír mé, is brat na béithe bailbhe i mo láimh agam.
Cheana féin tugann sí ar fuaid na cruinne mé gach oíche.
Ní gá dhomh ach an cogarnach ceart a chur ina cluais chlé:
'Mo ghraidhn do léim, a sheanabhéim *hoover,* a chailín,
Haí over to England, Haí over to Spain.'

And like the boy
and the wolf, I probably will not get away with it
much longer. Closing the door when the horse has bolted,
or something equally daft.

But why do you keep her, I hear you ask.
Because she is my hope and my only salvation.
The next time depression, that Wave of Tóime
sneaks up and crashes down on me, she will bring me clear back
to dry land, with the cloak of the dumb goddess in my hand.
Already she takes me around the world at night.
All I have to do is give the right whisper in her ear:
'Gee-up, you old lump of a hoover, you girl you,
Heigh-ho over to England, over to Spain.'

David Norris

Places of the Heart

It is 1986. This year I have not been to Jerusalem. It is the first time in many years that this has happened and when I saw those sturdy travellers from the south, the swallows, wheel and swoop the other evening over the Vico Road, I felt a tug at my heart. Something in the movement of the birds suggested a very different scene; not the leaden waters of Killiney Bay but Jerusalem, City of Gold, with the silver and gilt domes of its mosques glistening in the Mediterranean heat.

I think back to a Sunday morning in the late 1970s, walking on the ancient ramparts in the bright sunlight but with a heavy heart because my bags were already packed for the return to Dublin. Suddenly there was a subtle change in the light. Interposed between the walls and roofs of the old city and the sun, a cloud of storks homing from Egypt, wings outstretched and motionless in the buoyant air, hung and glided in perfect formation, their feathers filtering the harsh light. We halted in wonder at the sight. The ancients would have forged a myth of the inter-connecting worlds of the human, the animal and the divine from that moment, but inevitably the blare of horns dragged us back to everyday life.

For some reason the eve of departure frequently brought some such magical occurrence, perhaps due to the heightened nervous receptivity of anticipated leave-taking (I remember for example a moonbow observed one sleepless pre-flight midnight over Ramot), but whatever the cause, even laying aside the fact that the three great monotheistic religions have their roots there, Jerusalem is a mystic place.

A special magic makes Jerusalem for me a place of the heart. For surely if this phrase means anything at all, it means a place where emotional adolescence ends in the exchange of love. And so it was with me. Through the friendship of one man, I fell in love with the Levant and its peoples and embraced its life and culture, the romantic lure of the east even conquering my fear of flying. I remember clearly my first flight from London to Tel Aviv. We had to check in four or five hours before departure from Heathrow. I had a couple of pints to steady my nerves, and, during the hours preceding the flight, every time I went to the lavatory I was re-frisked by the El Al guard — tight was scarcely the word for the security!

Everything was strange to me: the kosher in-flight meals; the sturdy almost architectural character of the Hebrew language, in contrast to the flowing Arabic script of English, and the gruff, guttural masculinity of its accent; and then the Hassidic Jews, incongruous in the sophisticated modernity of a great flying machine. I had never seen people like them before, dressed in black gabardine, fur caps, untidy and wispy, with straggling cummerbunds, frayed bits of leather and string wrapping their unathletic bodies, eyes alert for heresy, mouths suddenly popping into a gabble of religious or dietary dispute. Yet it was they who provided a focus for the pent-up emotion of us passengers. The sun was behind us, dipping towards the horizon like an angry orange thrown by one of the old gods, when a vague rim of brown, baked land became apparent. As if by instinct the Hassids flocked to the point in the plane closest to land — their land — Eretz Israel, from which they had been banished for perhaps two thousand years. Anachronistic they may be, but as they began to chant they drew our sentiment towards them like scarecrow spirit-conductors.

A few minutes later we taxied to a halt and looking out of the window I could see the familiar international uniform of ground staff: overalls and earmuffs. But the faces under the baseball-style caps were Phoenician, skin as brown as their brown eyes and hair as black as the runway tar. The cabin door opened and a soft gush of warm air flowed up the steps — a breath of enchantment and the first real whisper from the face of the east.

Dazed, exhausted and a little tipsy from the evening warmth, I emerged scanning the crowd outside the barrier anxiously. I need not have worried. The face I wanted to see was there, trying to look solemn and composed but not even the hooded Iraqi lids could quench the delight in the eyes, and there was a smile that lit up the whole airport. We drove in a Sherut — the shared Mercedes limousine taxi service traditional between the larger cities of Israel — past shadowy palms and then onto a highway that curved gradually up towards the Jerusalem Hills.

My sole memory of that trip is of the electric proximity of Ezra wedged in beside me in the back seat. Now, of course, the Jerusalem Tel Aviv Highway is as familiar to me as the Bray Road — the graceful white arches of the monastery at Latrun marking the start of the climb to the Holy City itself, the pathetic shells of military vehicles from 1948 abandoned at the side of the road like childhood's Dinky toys and preserved in the mountain air as a permanent memorial to those who died in the birth pangs of the Israeli nation, fields of sunflowers gone to seed standing with blackened disconsolate faces and stooped shoulders like some terrible photograph from Yad Vashem, and the arthritically twisted limbs of the vines on their ancient terraces.

The first address I lived at in Jerusalem was on the fringes of the fashionable embassy district. Ezra had taken the lease on a little 'house' behind one of the exclusive apartment blocks. The house itself was tiny, the former washhouse of the apartments, built in the 1930s from Jerusalem stone, and about the size of a comfortable bathroom in suburban Dublin. It consisted of one room into which you stepped immediately from the garden and in this restricted space we conducted every aspect of our lives both intimate and social, cooking, talking, sleeping, entertaining friends. There was only one division of the space: a cubicle at the kitchen end of the room that contained a small hand-basin and flushing lavatory above which a rickety shower attachment hung perilously. Here you could quite literally have the Dublin man's dream — a shower, a shite and a shave, and all simultaneously.

I was happy, for here at last, after many years, I belonged again to a social unit, even if our family consisted of only two members, and when the first invitation addressed to the two of us as a couple arrived, my joy was complete. My duties consisted of hanging out the bedding to air under the pine trees in the morning, shaking pine needles off them in the late afternoon and making the bed, doing the washing-up and organising the household. I was a curious but contented mixture of Pasha and skivvy, for I also received my early morning coffee and copy of the *Jerusalem Post* (the main Israeli/ English language newspaper) out on the little terrace under the trees.

On my first visit I was timid about exploring on my own, particularly since I had no Hebrew, but at the confluence of Berlin Street and Azza Street stood a lozenge-shaped kiosk strategically placed behind a bus stop: Confisserie Marcelle. Here I could find a friendly refuge, exchanging memories of Paris in rusty French with Marcelle herself, a diminutive and twinkling exile from the Seine, barricaded behind trays of petits fours, ranks of confectionery in jars, and boxes of exotic chocolates.

The suburbs of Jerusalem have their own beauty: elegant, clean buildings and leafy gardens from which a sudden splash of colour shows red or purple from an exotic shrub, or higher up among the branches a yellow mist of mimosa spray, and over all the balm of evening bringing a scent of jasmine. Nevertheless, for me, as I suspect for many, the real Jerusalem is the old city itself, for this is really the Golden City of legend. Here the honey-coloured stone has absorbed sunlight for centuries until it almost glows in the dark. A confusing network of alleys criss-crosses the quarters — Armenian, Jewish, Christian and Arab — allowing the unwary to get lost between the Jaffa Gate, breached to provide a ceremonial opening for the visit of pompous Kaiser Wilhelm II in 1911, and the Damascus Gate, where you can sit in an Arab café smoking a nargilah or hookah while watching a gaggle of Hassids with long, gandery strides make for the Kotel or Wailing Wall.

We walked these alleyways many times, but seldom purchased anything except miniature cups of strong, aromatic Turkish coffee or some pebbles of incense from an ancient relic of

Ottoman days complete with red tarboosh, full of dusty courtesy in his cave near the Cardo. Our shopping we always did on Friday morning or early afternoon in the Mahane Yehuda, the ramshackle Jewish market behind Jaffa Street. What a confusion of vegetables, fruit and humans rioted along its narrow passages and stalls in preparation for every Sabbath! The visit to the Mahane Yehuda was a never-to-be-missed ritual, even after our move away from damp, dark Berlin Street to the bright, well-aired flat in Ramot.

Where Berlin Street was satisfyingly bohemian, Ramot had all the comforts of suburbia, but most precious of all was the sense of light, for Jerusalem is above all a city of light. How many evenings have I stood at our window in Ramot watching the light change from blue to purple, and then the forest-clad hills across the valley darken and begin to shimmer with discreet light from paths and scattered houses. From the kitchen window I could catch a glimpse in the distance of the last few buses leaving by the highway for Tel Aviv as the traffic stopped to observe the holy day. Then, after the meal and in the gentle light of candles, wearing the long flowing garments of the Hebron Arabs, we would listen to songs of love from Oum Khalsoom, Fairuz or Farid Al Atrache. As the years went by, I found myself as much at home in Jerusalem as in Dublin. Even now, when Ezra and I are apart, I find my thoughts returning there, and like a mirage the walls of the old city tufted with the mauve and white flowers of caper bushes rise before my eyes only to melt away again.

In my mind a potpourri of memories is stirred. Cool, white rooms in Nachlaot with high-domed ceilings and tiled floors. Little pads and pencils placed at the doorways of many Jerusalem dwellings, so that messages can be left and no visit is totally in vain (would they survive in Dublin, even in the suburbs?). Elaborate rituals of food and friendship. Sturdy ice-cream vendors stamping across the roasting sand of Tel Aviv shouting 'Arteek, Arteek, Leemone, Vaneell, Choco-Choco'. And stories, always stories, for the Jewish love a good tale. In a taxi, at a bus stop, queuing in the cookie shop, momentary intimacies are forged and life stories swapped.

I remember staying in a little hotel on Hayarkon Street in Tel Aviv. Breakfast one morning was interrupted by the intrusion of a young American, brash and born again, eager to share with us the gospel of his personal encounter with Christ. The only people at breakfast were an elderly couple and myself. The couple were polite and non-committal, but as a Christian I felt deeply embarrassed and when the evangelist left I apologised to the old man. He smiled gently, thanked me, and told me he had experienced much, much worse. He was born in Germany. He lived in Munich. He lost his mother, father, brother, sisters and first wife in World War II and had himself survived only by accident.

The Nazis came for them piecemeal and as he was the youngest, he was nearly the last. Re-living the story he expressed amazement at the way the family had lived; how in the middle of madness they tried to live a normal life. He recalled, 'the day that they came for my wife and myself, I was out at the dentist for a long-standing appointment. My dentist was a Dr Goering, cousin of the Reichs-Marschall. He continued treating Jews but they couldn't touch him. He told me to come back the next day for a filling. When I got home the Gestapo were waiting. They took me to the police compound where I was to be held awaiting transport to the camps. The next afternoon I was called out. I thought it was the end, but it was a messenger from the dentist. They gave me back my clothes. I was released for my appointment. The dentist said nothing. Once my filling was done I left the surgery and made straight for the station and got on the first train. I escaped. It was a miracle'.

An unbelievable tale, and yet looking at the old man and his second wife with their simple courtesy I knew it was true. Israel has many such stories and we are bound to listen. It is a place to which the heart is drawn inexorably.

Just a year ago I did go back. On my own. To be alone in Jerusalem was a strange, haunted feeling, like coming out into the sunlight from a cinema or waking from gas in an old-fashioned dentist's surgery. The buildings and the people were familiar, but both I and the way I saw them had changed in some irreversible frightening way.

Since I was a child I have always when abroad scoured the night sky for the friendly, reassuring figure of Orion the Hunter. On that visit he had abandoned my sky, which was now full of unfamiliar stars. I was sure it was an omen, and a black one at that. But I had not counted on the pre-departure miracles so often provided by Jerusalem, or perhaps I thought that my desolation had drained the magic from the entire city.

And then at 3.30 on the morning of my flight, as I left my bags to the gate for the taxi, suddenly, sandwiched between two tall buildings and lying on his side with one leg below the horizon as if he had just got up specially to say goodbye, was my old friend, the Hunter. So perhaps Isaac Singer was right when he wrote that no love of any kind is ever lost. Maybe the time will once more come when I will say to myself yet again, 'next year in Jerusalem'. And mean it.

Watching the Mountains in Tibet

Up there in the snow my past lies frozen
Clear and simple and sparkling.
As I look on its bright blankness I see
A summer afternoon — my mother's damasked dressing table,
Scent bottles casting a cut-glass lunch-time light.
Then bird-prints in a winter garden, while from back here
A speck in the snow might even be human,
Seeming to move, to stop, while the mind's eye designs,
discerns.
As the bus turns the corner, it all
Vanishes forever like childhood.

Lhasa/Tsethang, April 1997

Joyce in Zurich '78

Flowers in a cold hand placed,
The Fluntern cemetery.
How strange,
You always hated flowers, Nora, spaced
Swissly now with you, used to say.

Are you smiling to yourself down there?
Perhaps a spectral laugh escapes
Like coffin gas at your unplanned
Respectability in the Zurich air.

 **Denis O'Brien**

At the Reading in Waterstones

i. m. Michael Hartnett

Your ferrety vigilance had been swayed by the drink.
By the bookshelf, I handed you my loved copy
of *Selected Poems* for signing. 'To Dnns,' you scrawled,
missing the vowels and barely keeping your feet.

You were stumbling to a world of hard, hard consonants:
a building stripped down to a frame of steel girders;
the flesh on a body sinking through a skeleton;
the melody of poetry played harshly.

Lansdowne Road Haiku

I

9am:
on the sunny pavement
shadows of railings

*

leaves falling:
hordes from the DART
rushing to work

*

commuters gone —
for moments
the perfume of souls

*

5pm:
shadows of trees
swaying underfoot

II

September morning —
above the traffic
rustling in the trees

*

changing pavements:
big leaf patchwork
small leaf mosaic

*

by the road
a dead pigeon —
wind feeling for its wings

*

on the leafless road
the stadium
a presence for the winter

Snapshots: Ireland

morning traffic-jam:
a party balloon bounces
from bonnet to bonnet

halloween over —
inner city streets
clear of 'For Sale' signs

the new wing:
Zen garden on one side
Versailles on the other

April sun:
tax cuts
revealing more skin

at the tribunal
he curses the requisitioned IPA diary
for its pages too large

he leaves the tailor's shop
and becomes his shirts

Rush, Co. Dublin

From the top of a bus lurching
along the narrow roads of Rush,
the market garden of Ireland,
I see on one side vans, greenhouses,
fields of chives and cabbages;
on the other, an uneven graveyard,
its headstones faltering.

*

White-headed cabbages
unfolding their leaves
in packed row after row —
a wrinkling community.

*

Those vegetables with limp leaves and sandy roots
heaped up at the edge of a fresh brown field,
how many wellington-steps, barrow-metres, vehicle-miles
will it take to get them to a rack in somebody's kitchen?
I count in my head all the way back to the city.

42nd St, NY

The train rolls in. Grand Central. Sooty pillars and subway
        dullness.
Hundreds rush out, criss-cross, race over to the platform
        opposite
or pile onto the escalator for the exit. I step out
and my head screams with 'I Feel Good'.

                        *

I'm thumped on the shoulder
by an old lady waiting to cross Fifth Avenue.
'Isn't it great, isn't it great,' she bawls,
her eyes cocked to the news that's being fed
through her headphones, 'Hilary Clinton is flying out
to attend the funeral of Mother Teresa.'

                        *

I'm stuck in a bunch of people at the end of the block,
waiting for the pedestrian lights to say *walk*.
Around me: talk, traffic noise and scented hair.
The crowd pulls off and a voice on a megaphone breaks
from nowhere. A film roadie swings over us on a hydraulic arm.
'That's it now,' he commands, 'keep movin', keep movin'.
Look straight ahead. NOT AT THE CAMERA!'

Asian Rain

Hong Kong

Old men take birds for a walk to the park
and hook their cages on a branch
for ten minutes of song.

Sanur, Bali

Tied around squat statues
of Bali's grimacing gods —
skirts of chequered black and white:
good and evil held in balance,
waiting for a pawn to fall.

Two Haiku

A Balinese road
a tree frog misses its branch —
splat!

*

Along the dark road
squat Buddhas
laughing out candlelight.

Night Market, Bangkok

Just there, by neon-lit stalls, cluttered fakes,
throngs of touts pushing menus for sex,
a toddler is scrubbed and hosed down,
her arms around a tree, her chuckles going free.

Green from Space

I
Our Hong Kong guide, Jupiter Ku, a miss universe
of business with her petite blouse, skirt and mobile phone,
wants to know where we're from and when she hears
she exclaims, 'Oh Ireland! You love drinking so.
Please get taxi back to the hotel when you feel drunk.'

II
'Do you know our country?' I ask the Balinese doctor
whose next posting is 'Indonesian' East Timor. 'Ireland,'
he ponders, removing the syringe from the sterile wrapper.
'IRA, very brave men.' I look at him uneasily
as he tells me to turn in the bed and bare myself.
'Are you a member?' he enquires, jabbing me deftly.
I wait until he's finished before I set him straight.

III
I buy a Balinese mask of the good spirit Barong.
The hard-selling woodcarver takes up the credit card
and reads it. He smiles through a wrinkled face
and remembers how late one World Cup night
his whole village sat around a colour TV,
cheering on Ireland as they trounced the gods from Italy.

IV
The singing duo in the romantic Thai restaurant
ask us, the 'Happy Couple', for honeymoon requests.
I say, 'Have I Told You Lately' by Van Morrison,
and she, 'I Still Haven't Found What I'm Looking For' by U2.
They don't get the words but whine a global tune.

V
Drifting out further from parents, teachers, grocers,
writers, journalists, politicians, administrators,
factories, farms, towns and cities,
fields, rivers, mountains and lakes,
how green Ireland looks, how green from space.

The Lights of Charleville, 1951

The lights of Charleville couldn't come fast enough for Jim. He longed to be on that last stretch of road, about to give his wife, Kitty, an account of the day and his plans for expanding the forge. He also wanted to get in from the cold. The chilly night air inside the car was cooling his ears and nose, even his cheekbones, and the joints in his hands were beginning to twinge. There was a blanket lying on the back seat, but he wanted to save that for as long as possible. Snow was forecast.

He had left Cork over an hour before, so home wasn't too far off. Another three-quarters of an hour would see him in Charleville.

He shuffled on the seat and rubbed his coat vigorously, using the other hand to guide him round the turns on the road. When warmth came, it came like welcome company and he eased back, relaxing his shoulders. He observed how the headlamps of his black baby Ford hardly probed the night. More like hand torches, they lit up a few yards of winding road and cast shadows on the February ditches, giving them the look of witches or some other haunting thing.

As he focused on the patch of illuminated road moving towards him, memories of the day gradually surfaced. The engine, droning away beneath him, faded into the back of his mind. Soon he could no longer hear it.

His first stop that afternoon had been a visit to the docks in Cork to see iron brads arriving from England. There were seven or eight ships active when he arrived on the quay, each bustling with steaming winches, running wires and stevedores shouting and pointing directions as they off-loaded cargo. The sky was dull and dozens of low-flying seagulls wheeled around, screeching intrusively.

He sauntered along the noisy quay, avoiding both the stevedores rolling hand-trucks up and down the gangways and the horses and float-carts clanking over cobbles. He watched in awe at the speed at which winch-drivers hauled up cargo from hatches and swung it across on thick, rattling cables. Boxes, bags, crates and barrels were being landed with a heavy thud onto float-carts at intervals of one minute or so. The teamwork was breathtaking.

The cold didn't seem to bother the workers either. They wore thick jumpers and old trousers, and their foggy breath mingled casually with the sharp air.

Eventually he made it down to the end of the quay, where the ship from England was being off-loaded. The sudden recognition of the cargo gave him a rush of adrenaline. He stopped by the stone wall of an adjoining warehouse, comfortably out of the way, and looked around.

Hundreds of jute-coloured sacks sat squat on the cobbles, each poky looking as if it was stocked with disorderly bones. The boisterous dockers continued to land the remainder on the quay in a heavy-handed manner. It was no wonder a large number of sacks were ripped open or pierced by the spiky ends of the brads. It was an even bigger wonder no one was cut or stabbed by them.

Wall brads, eave brads, spur brads — the directory of imports from the Statistics Office in Dublin recorded that hundreds of thousands of pound's worth were being imported annually. And scanning the huddle of bags that had amassed in front of him, now being drawn away to a nearby warehouse, each bag holding half a gross at least, his calculations put the number of brads here at thousands. And this was just one day in one port. It seemed amazing that no one in the country was making them.

He stood for a good thirty minutes with his hands in his pockets, smiling to himself, thinking, observing, taking in the bustling scene, oblivious to his foggy breath or the cold settling on his bones. Seeing these imports made his decision to manufacture brads more real. It filled him with the hope and excitement of a new departure. His mind worked overtime. He compiled a list of hardware shops he would contact in the next week. He modified samples in his head and considered the right sizes and shapes. He worked out rough costs.

Finally, and with deep satisfaction, he inhaled the air and felt it run through him. He looked at his watch. Four o'clock. The evening was already closing in. It was time to head off for Galvin's hardware shop. He scanned the dock one last time and bounced off, rubbing his hands and smiling.

Galvin's was the largest hardware shop in the city and seemed like the best place to start making enquiries. It was located a few hundred yards from the docks, so he was there within minutes. He drove into the spacious yard and parked beside the timber stores. As soon as he opened the car door, the scent of freshly hewn wood met him. He breathed in deeply to let it circulate through his body, right out to his fingers and toes, and then made for the back door of the shop.

He entered a long and poorly lit room with dusty, congested shelves along the walls. An assistant and two builders in paint-spattered overalls were kneeling on the floor just inside the door. They were pouring paint from can to can and the pungent smell was almost overwhelming. Jim edged past them and looked up to the serving counter at the top to see if somebody was free.

A young, thin-faced assistant spotted him and waved him up. Usually he avoided the young fellows in hardware shops; they always got the order mixed up and tended to be too busy looking left and right over his shoulder. It didn't matter this time though. All he wanted was a few samples of brads, a few packets of welding rods and, of course, a chat with the owner, Mr Galvin.

Having placed the order, he walked towards Galvin, a small, pale-faced and grey-haired man in a beige work-coat who was busy spiking a docket from a previous customer. Without looking up, Galvin saluted him in his singing Cork accent.

'Cold oul' day.'

"Tis indeed then. Are you busy?'

'Not too bad at all now. Can't complain anyway.' Galvin pushed aside the docket book and leaned over the counter. His eyes met Jim's and he nodded.

'Sure I suppose it makes a change,' said Jim.

'Ah, it does.' Galvin hesitated slightly, 'I—I'm not too sure I know you at all. What line of work are—?'

'I've a forge there at the other end of the county.'

'Ah, is that so? Are you busy yourself?'

'Kept goin' anyway. Things could always be better, I suppose.'

'Couldn't they always. What has you down in these parts?'

Jim glanced down at the counter and smirked, 'Well now, I've somethin' that might interest you.'

'Is that right?' returned Galvin, perking up.

Jim looked up, 'I'm planning to go into makin' brads.'

He paused to see Galvin's reaction. Galvin was listening with his eyes.

'We're importin' enough of them anyway,' he continued, 'you know eave brads and the like.'

'By God we are. Sure aren't I doing it myself? I've a few thousand coming in now that you say it.'

'Do you think you might be interested in Irish ones?'

Galvin gave him a conspiratorial wink. 'Ah, I'm sure we might be able to do something all right.' Then he put in matter-of-factly, 'It's a policy of mine to buy Irish when it's on offer. How far are you into it?'

'A month or two off anyway. I've to jig up a few tools, to bend the iron and that.'

'Well, I have next month's order in already, but I'll reduce the one after to take some off you. And we can take things from there. Now, how's that?'

The assistant returned with the brads and rods and made for the docket book. Galvin nodded and raised his hand to indicate no charge. Jim was moved by his generosity. He pulled a pen from his jacket, wrote his name and address on a piece of paper and handed it to Galvin.

'That's great, Mr O'Brien,' said Galvin, looking at it. 'You know where we are anyway. Come on, I'll walk you out.'

Jim picked up his goods from the counter and strolled with Galvin down the narrow shop. There was an easy silence between them. They edged past the paint and out into the subdued daylight. A cold gust blew in from the east and they both shivered.

'Uh, that was a cold one,' Galvin commented, rubbing his hands. Then a thought struck him, 'Have you tried any other stores?'

'No, not yet,' Jim replied. 'Ah, I've been thinkin' about this for a few weeks. It's only now I've decided to go ahead.'

Jim guided their path towards his car, which looked tiny and box-shaped against the high wall of the hardware shop. He opened the door and placed the supplies on the floor at the back, then sat in and rolled down the window. Galvin leaned an arm over the roof.

'I'd say we're in for snow,' he announced, looking up.

Jim reached his head out, 'Looks like it indeed then.'

'Look, head away. You've a great idea. There's a lot of shoots and down-pipes needing brads now with all the building that's going on.' He added gravely, 'Just keep the fingers crossed that it doesn't slow down before it gets going, if you know what I mean.'

'I do indeed.'

'Go away before the weather turns. Get back to me soon with prices and numbers.'

Galvin knocked on the car roof and Jim pulled off for home.

To keep Kitty from worrying about him on the dark winter roads, Jim assured her that he wouldn't be too late. Still, it would be close to half past six by the time he got to Charleville. Baby Ben and the two toddlers, Jim óg and Jack, would probably be asleep, but Kitty would be finishing the housework, the wireless playing in the background for company.

He had not mentioned his intended visit to the docks before setting out for Cork after the midday meal. That was to be a part of tonight's surprise, when he would announce his new direction for the forge. Perhaps her response would be more relief than surprise. Once or twice, when they were eating dinner, he had mentioned that farmers were replacing cartwheels with pneumatic tyres. And he left it at that. She had got up from the dinner table and started putting things away quietly.

Thinking back, he was sure it was a year ago when he first saw the new style of cartwheel. It was Big Tom Reilly's cart that had received the remake and it was obvious that something was up a few days before the event. Reilly had got the cart newly painted red. And, one morning outside the creamery, the big man himself was off-loading galvanised milk tankards when Jim pulled up beside him and wound down the window.

'That band of yours needs adjustin',' Jim informed him, pointing to the slackening iron band on the cartwheel.

Reilly came round to look. 'Op, begod, it does then,' he agreed, seeming surprised, as if he didn't know or hadn't felt it.

A day or two later, Jim was throwing butcher hooks outside the forge when Reilly sped past on the new tyres. His stomach sank when he saw it. He felt disappointed, betrayed even. But a part of him admired the new poise of the outfit: the horse's proud and stocky trot, the red cart taking the weight with sureness and buoyancy.

It was only a matter of time before replacements like this became all the rage. And while it was true he would still have the workhorse shoes, plough and harrow repairs, farm gates and wrought iron railings, how long would they last? Even the shodding looked set to decline faster than he had anticipated. Outside the church recently, he had heard talk of how the tractor was becoming more affordable. Big Tom Reilly was one of the informed farmers.

Suddenly, Jim jolted forward with the car. The headlamps jumped and iron clinked in the back. He had hit a pothole.

His attention came back onto the road.

A few flakes of snow hit the windscreen. They were thick and fluffy and held on for moments. He watched them drip and remembered Galvin's forecast. This was the beginning of it all right. He reckoned that he had only a half an hour left and he hoped this wouldn't delay him.

More flakes swooned and veered towards the lights. Crosswinds began to blow the dots erratically in front of and over the car. The howling swirl made him more sensitive to the cold. He took one hand off the steering wheel and blew into it, feeling the rush of warmth along his palm. A wave of goose pimples tingled over him and he shuddered. He shook up his overcoat with his shoulders to generate more heat and crouched close to the steering wheel to save it as best he could.

The road was so dry that the snow lodged quickly. It drizzled its white over the ditches. It drifted into the corners of the windscreen and, bit by bit, built up on the glass like grey lacework. He flicked the switch for the wiper and waited for air to shoot from the manifold in the engine.

The wiper didn't budge. He turned it off and tried again. Nothing.

His view was almost obscured now. He slowed down to twenty miles an hour to allow more pressurised air to build up, something he often did to increase the speed of the wiper during heavy rain.

Again, the wiper wouldn't budge. He tutted and pulled up by the ditch. As he opened the door, the blustery wind blew snow in around the car. He tucked his chin into his chest and cleaned the windscreen with the back of his hand.

This regular stopping was going to be tiresome, he thought wearily as he got back in. But what else could he expect? The car had been more than ten years old when he bought it over a year before. Worse still, like so much of Ireland, it had been locked up in a shed during the war.

The snow was falling heavily now and the covering on the windscreen made it difficult to see again. He peered hard into the illuminated flurry and shook his head in disgust as he drove off.

Then, unexpectedly, the wiper jerked. He had left it switched on. He urged it to move further and it swung over, swiping the windscreen clean. He sighed with relief.

It must have been the manifold, faulty or something, taking longer to build up with pressure, he said to himself as he picked up speed again over the narrow, white carpet of snow.

The visibility, though, was short-lived. The snow, criss-crossing chaotically in front of him, laid another grey layer on the windscreen. He continued for a minute or so, until it was time for the same rigmarole. He took pressure off the accelerator and slowed down, down, down, until he was scarcely moving. The wiper stirred and pushed the snow across. It stopped, as if gasping for air, then made it back.

He would never get home at this rate, he thought. He had to do something else. A feeling of frustration and impatience gripped him.

He drove until the windscreen darkened and then decided to continue on by gauging his distance from the ditch on both sides. He looked left to make sure he was skimming close to the ditch. Then right to make sure it remained distant.

Over and back he looked, while stealing glances in front of him for sudden light. It was like driving through a tunnel, only glimmers escaping back from the headlamps to illuminate the sweeping ditch.

This was much better. He was getting home.

A minute or two later, he eased off the accelerator. There was no point in being reckless. Besides, he felt dizzy. The wiper cleared the window and revealed a fresh image of swirling snow. For a moment, an after-image from the moving ditch made the scene in front of him slide sideways.

He accelerated again. As a new layer of snow gathered on the glass, he thought he spotted lights in the distance. He drew closer to the steering wheel. They were lights all right, twinkling vaguely in the snowy darkness. There seemed to be two of them.

The lights of Charleville. At last. His first welcome home.

He would soon be there.

The faintly lit speed-clock on the dash read thirty, but his driving seemed faster. He kept an eye on the ditch on his left and careered towards the town. He looked right to make sure he wasn't veering too far onto the other side of the road. As he turned back, his eye caught a faint glow on the windscreen. He couldn't be near the town this soon, could he?

He drove on, perplexed, slightly anxious, noting his distance from the sweeping ditch and shooting glances in front of him. The glow got stronger.

Something was definitely approaching. And fast.

He pulled his foot from the accelerator and flicked the switch for the wiper.

Nothing happened.

He panicked. He looked left, then right. He seemed close to the ditch on the other side of the road. He looked left to check. He wasn't sure.

The glow was almost on top of him.

He hurried the wiper, 'Come on, come on.'

The wiper was dead.

He looked sideways. Then at the glaring windscreen. 'Come on, come on.'

The wiper stirred. It swept the window clean and the lights of an oncoming car dazzled him. He was on the wrong side of the road.

He put his foot down and swung left.

The oncoming car sped past, beeping. He glimpsed the driver's angry hand working the air, his poorly lit face grimacing with fury. The driver had had no intention of stopping.

He felt dizzy. His heart slipped and hammered. He pulled in to the side of the road and sat in near darkness, shivering. He began to flush and shake and his breathing got louder. The windscreen snowed up like a coffin lid, letting less and less light through.

There were a few minutes of blankness, of nothing but him sitting still: no past, no future, no present. Then, the wiper started all on its own, swinging over and back. He jerked his head and looked at it in disbelief. After a few swings it stopped.

He heard again the sound of the engine ticking over. He reached back for the blanket and covered his legs. He took a deep breath and pulled out, crouching on the steering wheel to impose himself on the wild snowy road. The muscles in his shoulders were knotted. His perceptions were heightened. He found himself focusing on aspects of the scene ahead: the way each snaking bend opened up a new length of faintly lit road; the way the white, thorny and exacting ditches loomed along the sides; the way the large winter trees held up austere arms in detached supplication or terror.

His plans were falling back into silence. He knew now that Kitty would have to wait for another time to hear them. What he wanted was space, a space by the fireside in which to thaw out and gradually respond to the coaxing of Kitty's searching words, her concerned fingertips on his shoulders.

Two lights appeared in the distance. The lights of Charleville. The real lights.

He drove a little towards them and stopped to let the wiper work, drove some more and stopped again, and again, and again, the flurry of snow blowing against his longing for home, his longing for home divided between driving blind and stopping to see.

Gerald Dawe

Border-Crossing: Nationality and Place in 1999

I live in a town called Dún Laoghaire, south of Dublin. The town, amongst other things, is a well-known ferry port, which was once called Kingstown. During the nineteenth century it played host to various members of the British monarchy, including King George IV in 1821, and in 1906 the entire Atlantic fleet of the Royal Navy lay in anchor. In 1920, two years before the Irish Free State was established, Kingstown became Dún Laoghaire, a name recalling the fifth-century king who reputedly lived in the area. Since independence from Britain, or the Westminster jurisdiction, Dún Laoghaire has seen hundreds of thousands of Irish men and women leave the port for England and further afield in search of work. That pattern, with rises and falls from the 1950s up to the early 1980s, started to change in the 1990s.

The ferry terminal has been transformed from the draughty sheds it once consisted of into an attractive and artful reception area, through which tourists flood in their thousands. They travel on state-of-the-art, high-speed ferries the size of grand palaces, which shoot across the sixty-four miles (100 km) between one shore (Holyhead in Wales) and the Irish coast in jig time.

Facing the old terrace that once looked down upon the bay, an extensive development is taking place, on the site of a once famous dancehall called the Pavilion, which in turn is overlooked by the Royal Marine Hotel. This development is of apartments (mostly sold off the architect's plans), retail units and a 300-seat theatre. It looks quite good, with an appropriate maritime theme. I walk past it every day. Further up the terrace there is a Roman Catholic church surrounded by a low wall. On this wall sit, at different times of the day, young, unemployed men and women, many of whom have children, waiting to attend a drug rehabilitation unit in the town centre. They are angry, lost, and have very little hope in the world. The church behind them is attended mostly by senior citizens, and by dutiful families at weekends. Across the road from where these kids sit, smoke and talk incessantly to each other at an incredible speed and drawl, two refugees play music outside a first-generation shopping centre; one on an accordion, joined occasionally by another who plays the trumpet. They are Albanians or Romanians, I am not sure which, and I did not want to ask them in case they got the wrong message.

Each month hundreds of refugees arrive in Ireland. When they are not fighting for a place outside the understaffed, over-pressed office that has lately been opened to process their applications for residency in Ireland, these people, like the two musicians, will stand on the corner, metaphorically speaking, looking at what is going on around them. They will see a society that is one of the most prosperous in Europe; where investment is unparalleled since the foundation of the state in 1922; where, if one looks back over the quarter of a century to 1972 when Ireland joined what was then called the Common Market, the standard of living and quality of life for the majority of its citizens has improved beyond their wildest dreams.

In that quarter of a century of Irish history the following has happened: after twenty-five years of an intimate, intense and dirty sectarian war of cultural attrition, the ideology of the Irish state has been completely revised and awaits agreement in the north before seceding one of the core values and aspirations of this country, a move overwhelmingly endorsed by the people in the referendum of 1998; the once all-powerful Roman Catholic Church has undergone a profound and irreparable loss of social control; the imperative sense of 'Irishness', which previous generations had held on to so dearly (almost piously), has evaporated into a much more relaxed and energetic consciousness of being 'European'. No longer transfixed by not being English, the younger generation in Ireland, the European generation if you like, born in the early 1970s, are moving into positions of power throughout the Irish state, in the European Parliament and Commission and, of course, throughout the entire landscape of academic, media, business and other professional worlds. Their liberated (and liberating) sense of nationality, citizenship and place is both exhilarating and worrying by turn, and I would like to explore this contradiction for two reasons. First, because I identify with it very much myself, even though I am twenty years older; and second, because in this developing, enlarging, expanding Europe I also harbour an anxiety about those who are being left behind (like those kids on the church wall) and I am concerned about the cultural engine driving enlargement.

If traditional Ireland is breaking up, and we hear about this every day on the radio and television, the impact should be most keenly reflected in the way that people see themselves. Ireland, described by the literary scholar and critic, James Mays, as 'a country with a small homogenous population at the edge of a continent', can be seen as a paradigm for the fate of other smaller countries in the European context.

With a complex and complicated colonial history, assimilated in part to the Imperial past but also mightily defiant of it; with a distinctive and powerful, non-metropolitan culture in its folk traditions; with an urban, modernist literature personified by James Joyce and Samuel Beckett, who redefined the meaning of literary art; with a powerful and presently thriving minority language (Gaelic); with a provocatively, and at times violently, independent-

minded Protestant minority mostly living in the northern province
— this brilliant, contrary, variable world has made it possible for
people born in Ireland to invent themselves, rather than be
snapped shut into a box of inherited national definition. I see no
reason why this sense of fluidity cannot play across the national
borders of those re-emerging states of Europe, as they break out
of the cold chill of communism and rediscover their old histories,
the alignments of the past crossing with new-found political or
cultural alliances.

Ireland's economic and social gains since 1973, when entry
to the Common Market took effect, have been immense. Ireland
has seen a blossoming of the indigenous culture and the erosion
of some very dusty ideals from the earlier part of the twentieth
century; it has seen the floodlighting of issues of justice, which
traditional political and social practice in Ireland had kept either
silent or silenced. Legislation in regards to women's health,
contraception and divorce, legalisation of homosexuality, fair
employment and anti-discrimination laws, have all passed through
the relevant government agencies and jurisprudence because of
the European Union. The EU, in effect, became a guarantor of civil
rights and civic space; it oxygenised the Irish state and made
available another 'impartial' avenue of redress and perspective to
people who may have felt, in the intimate, provincial familiarities
of Irish life, uncomfortable with pursuing issues locally or even
nationally.

But, as in all things, there is a downside, and I see this
particularly in cultural terms. Much has to do with the marketing
mantras of post-industrial, corporate capitalism. If financial
services become, ultimately, our god, and we golf our way to
heaven, it seems to me that enlargement will effectively mean only
one thing: economy. Culture as economy, economy as culture.
Was Marx bizarrely right after all? The superficiality of some such
phrase as 'the Celtic Tiger' will merely be transported some place
else, when the time comes, to Slovakia or Slovenia, perhaps to
Montenegro. Never mind the place, how is it for mobile phones
and digital TV? A vigilant EU must guarantee that the essential and
necessary deference to national cultural experience, distinctive
histories, sensibilities and architecture, both physical and moral,
should not be over-ridden by unthinking or one-track corporate
ambition. It also seems that the political and cultural meaning of
enlargement has to be explained, not explained away. That the
benefits as much as the burden should be spread equally among
the peoples of Europe, many of whom are becoming increasingly
unsure of how the EU (as it currently is, never mind how it might
be) actually relates to their everyday individual life, here and now.
Eaten bread, I hear an ancestral voice whisper, is soon forgotten.

On the wider scale a key question remains: is there a

common vision, which the EU can develop out of the marvellously multicultural world from which Europe, if 'it' exists at all, is made?

Historically, poets in Ireland dutifully attended the courts of their lords and ladies with words of praise and not-so-coded words of question and care. I will finish therefore with a poem, which recounts a journey, an apocryphal journey, which my own forebears took from different parts of Europe. My great-grand-father's people from Huguenot France; my great-grandmother's people from we know not where in central Europe; both marrying in Belfast early in the nineteenth century.

The poem is named after my great grandmother, whose maiden name was Quartz, and in it I address her own people's experience as they crossed all kinds of borders, inner and outer, and entered, as so many are doing throughout Europe, a new world, a new language, a new enlarged place.

Quartz

for Katrina Goldstone

So there is something I want to know,
great-grandmother, reclining on whichever
foreign shore or ambrosial meadow,
taking a second look at the old place —

the valiant village, the provincial district,
the back-breaking hill-climb to the apartment,
the quiet evening square in this country town
or that frontier post, down by the coastal resort

of some famous lake, say, with Roman baths,
or a minority language — I want to know
who your grand dame was, or paterfamilias,
disembarking in a draughty shed, thinking

Liverpool or Belfast was really New York,
blinking in the greyish light of a noisy dawn,
looking out for rooming houses, a decent hotel,
putting one foot in front of the other,

taking the first right and walking, walking,
past the shipping offices and custom houses,
the rattling trams and carters and mill girls,
the steep factories and squat churches till the hills

converge upon this three-storied terrace
with the curtains drawn, the bell-pull shining,
and you pull the bell-pull and in whatever
English you'd learned you stepped in.

Thomas Kinsella

Brothers in the Craft

In the creative generations there is often
a conspiracy of the mature and the brilliant young;
a taking in hand, in hopes of a handing on.

In the elder, an impulse against that settled state
when the elements work in balance against each other
in worn stability, no longer questioned;

to borrow something out of the restlessnesses
of the half ready, confide an ethereal itch
into new, committed fingers.

                    In the other,
a self-elect asking only to watch
— even be let hold something — the imbalance of growth.

These settle in the medium in their turn,
a part of the lasting colour of the work
taken from the early accidental particulars.

Again and again, in the Fifties, 'we' attended
Austin Clarke. He murmured in mild malice
and directed his knife-glance curiously amongst us.

Out in the dark, on a tree branch near the Bridge,
the animus of Yeats perched.
                    Another part of the City,
Tonio Kroeger, malodorous, prowled Inchicore.

At the Western Ocean's Edge

Hero as liberator. There is also
the warrior marked by Fate, who overmasters
every enemy in the known world
until the elements reveal themselves.
And one, finding the foe inside his head,
who turned the struggle outward, against the sea.

Yeats discovered him through Lady Gregory,
and found him helpful as a second shadow
in his own sour duel with the middle classes.
He grew to know him well in his own right
— mental strife; renewal in reverse;
emotional response; the revelation.

Aogan O Rathaille felt their forces meeting
at the Western ocean's edge
— the energy of chaos and a shaping
counter-energy in throes of balance;
the gale wailing inland off the water
arousing a voice responding in his head,

storming back at the waves with their own force
in a posture of refusal, beggar rags
in tatters in a tempest of particulars.
A battered figure.
                          Any force remaining
held on waves of threat inside the mind.

As who can not confirm, that set his face
beyond the ninth shadow, into dead calm.
Dame Kindness, her bowels torn.
The stranger waiting on the steel horizon.

The Last

Standing stone still on the path, with long pale chin
    under a broad-brimmed hat, and aged eyes
staring down Baggot Street across his stick.
    Jack Yeats. The last.

Upright, stately and blind, and hesitating
    solitary on the lavatory floor
after the Government meeting down the hall.
    De Valera. The last.

Politics of the Dual Tradition

Speaking in Brussels on 20 September 1988, Margaret Thatcher, the British prime minister, referred to the common experience of the major European countries: 'the story of how Europeans explored and colonized and — yes, without apology — civilized much of the world is an extraordinary tale of talent and valour', speaking of the processes of colonisation and empire (with some hesitation, but urging herself on) as of a job well done.

Jonathan Swift would have agreed with her, taking it — as in his 'Humble Address' — that 'to civilize the poorer sort of our natives' means 'introducing among them our language and customs'. And Thatcher would have agreed with Swift in dealing with the Irish, however civilised, as 'natives' still. She ruled out a United States of Europe in the same speech, because the EU member states must remain sovereign and independent. But she was thinking of the explorers and colonisers: 'Europe will be stronger precisely because it has France as France, Spain as Spain, Britain as Britain, each with its own customs, traditions and identity'.

Ireland was the closest of England's colonies, and the most thoroughly civilised. The mechanics of colonialism were tested in Ireland and the stages recorded in Irish literature, in both languages. It is one of the findings of Ireland's dual tradition that an empire is a passing thing, but that a colony is not. The explorers and colonisers, with the 'love and torrent of power' observed by Swift, can be got rid of with difficulty and bitterness, leaving a heritage of civil war and division. But through all the stages of settlement and change, with civil war or without, a colony establishes an independent life, with a confusion of loyalties that shows itself in politics and literature, manners and customs, and other things.

Not the least of these is a difficulty with definitions. It is a marginal area, and definitions can seem unimportant. But it is at the margin that the need for precision increases, and where things may be learnt.

In the *Oxford Anthology of English Poetry,* edited by John Wain, the editorial selection is made 'taking the word "English" to refer to the language more than to the nationality, and remembering that many of the most famous poets bred in these islands have been Scottish, Welsh or Irish . . .'. But the question of nationality insists and, finally, 'every poem . . . is by a poet who was or is a native, or at any rate a citizen, of "Britain" . . . I am confined to gathering native flora . . .'. Qualification can be a technical matter. It is noted that T. S. Eliot took British citizenship in 1927; other Americans are excluded: 'we no longer think of American poetry as virtually symbiotic with English. The two literary traditions have moved decisively apart . . .'. Some Irish poets are included; in the twentieth century W. B. Yeats and Seamus Heaney — Yeats presumably as a native of the pre-revolutionary United Kingdom; Heaney presumably as a native of Northern Ireland. Although, with the shifting of definitions, this is not clear. Elsewhere in the Introduction, the selection is described as 'being "limited" to the poetry of the British Isles'. In which case the exclusion of J. M. Synge or Samuel Beckett might be an act of judgement. Likewise the inclusion, in the selection from the nineteenth century, of 'The Shandon Bells', 'The Minstrel Boy', 'She is Far from the Land', 'Four Ducks on a Pond', and other old favourites.

For an Irish writer the matter of definition still arises, with the post-colonial confusions. Invited to contribute to an anthology of British poetry and replying to say that he does not belong, he can be assured that Irish is included under 'British'. Writing to disagree, he will be dismissed as troublesome. British editors are usually unwilling to accommodate the point. Seamus Heaney wrote a verse response, in his loosest verse, on being invited to contribute to a *Penguin Book of Contemporary British Verse*. He refused, and drew the line

> At being robbed of what is mine,
> My *patria*, my deep design
> >   To be at home
> In my own place and dwell within
> >   Its proper name
> . . . British, no, the name's not right . . .
> >   ('An Open Letter', 1983).

But Heaney has accepted an Eric Gregory Award, given for the encouragement of young British poets; applicants must be British by birth. Other Northern Irish writers have done the same. A Belfast bookshop can advertise an 'Excellent selection of Poetry books by Irish Authors' in a Belfast literary review, and list poets only from Northern Ireland. An article on 'The Imaginary Irish Peasant' in the October 1991 *PMLA*, listing *en passant* the names of the directors of the Field Day enterprise ('all from Northern Ireland'), omits the name of the director born in Kilkenny. But there is more a provincial than a colonial air to some of this. ('The province' is a unionist term for Northern Ireland.)

A great deal of poetry has been published in recent years by poets from the province of Northern Ireland, and a great deal of attention has been paid to it. There is an impression that the 'Troubles', deplorable in other ways, have given rise to a creative response among the poets amounting virtually to a renaissance. A renaissance not altogether unprepared for. There has long been a distinctive poetry in Northern Ireland, characterised in a review of 11 April 1992, in *The Irish Times*, by 'formal and moral austerity' as against the 'dreamy self-satisfaction somewhere between innocence and smugness — a recurring feature of Southern verse'. In the recent past there were Louis MacNeice and others, with MacNeice adopted as a 'patron' of the renaissance; in the nineteenth century Sir Samuel Ferguson and others; and others before that, from the beginnings of Anglo-Irish poetry in the seventeenth century. Some have gone further, pointing to a separate Ulster tradition in Gaelic literature.

The idea has an appearance of completeness, but this is achieved by uncritical inclusion and programmatic exclusion. 'Northern poetry' is a journalistic entity rather than a literary one, and with features of propaganda more than of journalism. It adds a literary argument to the arguments for an 'Ulster' naturally separate within Ireland. But it is an Ulster of six counties, with the three non-unionist Ulster counties edited out. Even poetry can have political weight for a community attending fiercely to its borders, where the position of the border, or its existence, is subject to argument and where pressures are abnormally high. A willingness among the writers to take advantage of the general attention is understandable.

A renaissance of some kind in Northern Ireland, some interaction of art with the significant violent reality, would not be surprising given adequate talents concerned and active. Intense events are happening, involving long-standing caste supremacy and injustice, frustrated protest, exemplary heroism and meanness, and other noteworthy human behaviour. It would not be the first time that poetry in Ireland had responded to social and political change in an important way, so that the times would later prove hard to understand fully without an understanding of the poetry, or the poetry without an understanding of the times. The phases of Norman invasion and settlement were accompanied by a vital poetic commentary in Irish. At the close of the seventeenth century, with the expulsion of the patrons of bardic poetry, a number of bardic poets accustomed to the inherited function of political and social comment produced a body of major poetry to accompany their own extinction. From the seventeenth century to the nineteenth century, great folk song and poetry in Irish, and ballads in English, responded to the violence of the times with lasting emblems blending the imagery of politics and love. In the nineteenth century the custodians of the Irish poetic tradition in English, as Yeats identified them — Davis, Mangan and Ferguson, commented in different intensities on the nationalist feeling of the time and provided the beginnings of a real renaissance in poetry and drama.

So there are precedents for a poetic response to the violence of the time. But a renaissance on the suggested lines would have an imposed and consciously structured basis, separating a part out from the political, social and literary whole and providing for it an isolated present and an adjusted past. A phase in the process can be seen in Terence Brown's *Northern Voices: Poets from Ulster* (1975). The selections begin with Samuel Ferguson and end with four new voices of the time, including Seamus Heaney and Derek Mahon. Brown sees the poets in his survey as contributing 'not to a separate Ulster poetic tradition but to Anglo-Irish and/or British Poetry' and as addressing a primary audience outside Ulster. But they were all 'either born or raised in the North of Ireland', and the book sets out to read their work with their Ulster background 'firmly in mind'. Ulster was 'a distinctive Irish region, at least since the seventeenth century' and it is felt that an intelligent reading of these poets requires an awareness of this. Common thematic patterns and poetic concerns show themselves in their work because 'the social and historical realities of their native province' affect them all. But much of the pattern-finding that follows is based on dubious data; the book's company of modern northern poets is filled out with writers whose poetry would be of provincial interest at best, while a related larger unity is going unrepresented.

During one of the periods covered by Brown's book, Austin Clarke and Patrick Kavanagh — neither of them born or raised in Northern Ireland — dealt with topics relevant to an understanding of Ireland as a divided country: the politics of the Civil War in some of Clarke's best poetry, and a social element in both poets. Brown's more recent book *Ireland: A Social and Cultural History* (1981) shows that he has been made aware of the larger unity. In it he refers to 'the terrible inheritance of the civil war which followed the Treaty of 1921'; to 'a small country made disastrously smaller by a border that had set six of its counties adrift'; and to the remaining twenty-six counties where, in a devious interpretation, 'the field lay open therefore for the Catholic nationalist majority to express its social and cultural will unimpeded by significant opposition from powerful minorities'. There is no comment on the transformation of the unionist minority in the north, by the same act, into a supremacist permanent majority which proceeded, in the name of democracy, to discriminate methodically against the newly created nationalist minority. This was in fact the purpose behind partition, establishing Northern Ireland in its present, self-destructive state. But no matter how one interprets the political events, a selection of the significant poetry of the period that claims to indicate anything more than the provincial could not limit itself to the poetry from Ulster.

Conditions in the north of Ireland from the 1930s to the 1950s might have been dealt with by a major poet. It is not clear if Louis MacNeice, born in Northern Ireland, had the capacity. But he withdrew from Ireland, and from the topic, into the British poetry of his time. There is only an occasional backward look. It is possible that this withdrawal, or refusal, had an effect on the overall quality of MacNeice's achievement: certainly MacNeice — least provincial of men — would have been uneasy, on the evidence of his work, at being chosen as patron of an Ulster branch of modern British verse.

In the late 1960s and early 1970s the injustices in the northern state, no longer quietly accepted, started a kind of civil war. The years since then, in Britain and Northern Ireland, have been full of the rhetoric of anti-terrorism but empty of the consideration of causes. Poetry in Northern Ireland, far from constituting a renaissance, has responded to nothing in and contributed nothing to the situation. Nor is there any reason why it should. There are things more urgent than the political or social scene when the poetic agenda requires. And the poetry of Derek Mahon or Seamus Heaney is for the most part concerned with other things.

The values of Mahon's poetry are wide, and directed inward. In a bad time for the world he is taking cover and guarding a few basics. Heaney has dealt with some experiences of growing up Catholic in a Protestant, unionist six counties. The impression is of carefulness, fulfilling the established expectations — as one might expect from a member of the underprivileged class managing a successful exit. On the issues or the merits there is only what can be deduced from a few indirect comments made with one eye over the shoulder, 'feeling . . . that, as usual, I had . . . failed an obligation' and 'shying as usual'. This carefulness is excused in *Station Island* — carefully, with the words placed, ill fitting, in the mouth of Joyce's ghost:

> That subject people stuff is a cod's game . . .

> You lose more of yourself than you redeem
> doing the decent thing.

The ghost offers a friendly, positive suggestion, 'Stay hungry as you are. Get dangerous'. But this recommendation has not so far been adopted.

Apart from Heaney and Mahon, the poetry in Northern Ireland, and especially the commentary, has a minority air, isolated and truculent: the air of a colony that has been left to look after itself and of the colonial at home nowhere. Perhaps the strongest

single element is a failure of identity. John Hewitt, in his edition of
Allingham's poems, writes of Allingham as one of the Protestant
colonial minority after the Union for whom 'Ireland had ceased to
be a country and England was not theirs'.

The poetry of opinion is demanding, requiring the character
and capacity of Pope or Auden, the strength behind the prejudice
of Swift or Yeats. Hewitt's poetry is lacking on these levels, but
some of it is valuable for its complete presentation, in a
determined pentameter, of the colonial mentality. Speaking for the
colonist:

> We are not native here or anywhere.
> We were . . . left stranded here
> ('Ireland')

against the colonised:

> much I cherish lies outside their vision,
> and much they prize I have no claim to share
> ('The Scar')

assuming the voice of the dispossessed:

> . . . the sick, guilt-clotted legend
> of my creed-haunted, Godforsaken race
>
> . . . a people endlessly betrayed
> by our own weakness . . .
>
> . . . fables
> which gave us martyrs when we needed men
> ('An Irishman in Coventry').

Hewitt's allegorical poem 'The Colony' has the structure complete, the colonists looking out at the 'barbarian tribesmen' as they
'slither down' out of the hills ('the sullen Irish limping to the hills'
of Hewitt's poem 'Once Alien Here'; 'the Irish . . . out there
waiting, in sullen discontent, to take over' in Lord Clare's words,
at the setting up of the Union):

> They worship Heaven strangely, having rites
> we snigger at . . .
>
> . . . cunning by nature, never to be trusted,
> given to dancing and a kind of song
> seductive to the ear, a whining sorrow.
> Also they breed like flies . . .

The poem is aware of the principal injustice, dispossession: 'We took the kindlier soils. It had been theirs'; but justifies this by the colonist's natural superiority:

> We laboured hard and stubborn . . .
> till half the country took its shape from us.
> . . . we made it fat for human use

and disposes of any remaining guilt, and of any impulse toward reparation, with a condescending righteousness:

> I think these natives human . . .
>
>   . . . to be redeemed
> if they themselves rise up against the spells
> and fears their celibates surround them with
>   . . . would make amends
> by fraternising, by small friendly gestures
>
> Teams of the tamer natives we employed
> . . . but did not call them slaves.
> Some say this was our error. Others claim
> we were too slow to make them citizens.

The topic is finally discarded in the maintenance of prejudice: 'This is a matter for historians'. But Hewitt's colonists see that the days of empire are numbered and there is an element of worry. Some of them:

> . . . make common cause with the natives, in their hearts
> hoping to win a truce when the tribes assert
> their ancient right and take what once was theirs.

They settle, finally, for a common predicament with the colonised: 'this is our country also, no-where else'.

It is the dual state of things: the sullen Irish, dispossessed but refusing to disappear; and the self-righteous colonist, high and dry. They would both like things to be different: the dispossessed back in possession, the invader really at home. Facing the facts, they are left with each other. Whatever their differences, they are left with a shared reality. A capable critical assessment and editing of their literatures, as they deal with their experience, could reduce these differences or help to make them manageable. The effort would need to increase as the areas of difference narrowed, exposing more of the cherished fixations of nationalism or loyalty. And it would need an act of unlikely generosity to adjust some of the established structures. Finally the effort could prove too much.

*

John Hewitt inherits and accepts the role of the determined colonist. He knows that it cannot go on as it is but he refuses any dealings with the native tribes — sniggering at them, clowns no matter how dangerous. He finds the difficult first step impossible: acceptance of guilt with its obligations. A first step out of provincial isolation could seem easier if it was understood that it need not involve the abandonment of prejudice. Swift cherished his prejudices, but tried not to change the facts to fit; he reacted to particular injustices. Much of the nationalistic activity in Irish history is the same. It is less a matter of political ideals, or even the desire for a just society, than the violent ad hoc reaction to injustices no longer tolerable.

Terence Brown is one of Hewitt's colonists and has confessed himself one of 'those purists who were happier with the state of quarantine in which the two linguistic traditions existed until very recently' in Ireland. But he apparently accepts that the quarantine is ended and seems capable of the necessary first step. He has shown signs of openness and a preliminary understanding. Introducing the poetry of 1930 to 1965 in *The Field Day Anthology of Irish Writing*, he is clear about the society in which John Hewitt and W. R. Rodgers found themselves — a 'Northern Ireland of unionist misrule, British misgovernment and sectarian division'. Reviewing John Wilson Foster's *Colonial Consequences: Essays in Irish Literature and Culture,* he has written: 'Atavism is shockingly admitted ('We have approved discrimination and the codification of injustice; we have contemplated atrocity'). Yet Foster can get to the heart of things . . .'.

Brown himself is shocked that discrimination and injustice should be admitted, and moves on quickly. But he has recorded the reaction. Later in the review he refers, with no qualifying comment, to Foster's description of contemporary Northern Ireland as 'heir to a culture without apparent resource, a culture infected with noxious hatreds and provincial fatuities'; and, with emotional approval, to the possibility (unthinkable to Hewitt's colonists) that Northern Ireland's unionists, with

> . . . their 'old Britishness . . . mortally wounded', may find a way to what Foster identifies as 'wholeness without mystique' in which they can discover 'the confidence to extend generosity, to leave the refuge and prison that sectarianism is'. Speed the day.

From either standpoint within the tradition, colonised or colonist, their literatures in quarantine from each other or not, there are difficulties in accepting the whole: but it is apparent that it can be done.

Michael Mulreany

Markey Robinson

In January 1999, in a small house in Tudor Place, off Belfast's Crumlin Road, Markey Robinson died just days short of his eighty-first birthday. He had been an artist for almost sixty years, in which time he created a sprawling oeuvre. In the process he infuriated traditionalists, divided critics, refused to toe any official line, exasperated his supporters and, of course, delighted the art-buying public.

At the time of his death, Markey's status was unsure. His last major exhibition, in 1997, was largely unreviewed. This is not surprising: a late survivor of a previous generation, he was an isolated figure in an age of video art, multimedia and installation; of hard-edged styles and the urge to shock. Unloved by cultural bureaucrats and institutionally neglected, Markey Robinson had passed from critical view.

What comment was made, tended to be unflattering. In 1988, Brian Fallon in *The Irish Times*, fully dismissive, felt he could say nothing good about Markey's work. A few years later, Patrick Gallagher in *The Sunday Independent*, saw Markey in the mould of a popular singer. In the 1990s, critics re-discovering the primitive virtues of Dixon and Wallis overlooked Markey.

Other critics had other opinions. John Hewitt, in 1951, hailed Markey as 'Ulster's greatest primitive', considerable praise from the most important critic in a region that produced many of the great 'modern' Irish artists. Indeed, during the 1950s, Markey was favourably reviewed in serious French art journals. Huon Mallalieu, writing in *Country Life* in 1999, after Markey's death, felt he was 'reminiscent of Vlaminck but without the latter's rather sickly finish'. Markey, though never a likely *Country Life* reader, would have enjoyed this comparison with one of the painters who influenced his style. But mostly he was unconcerned with critics; he reciprocated their indifference and floated weightlessly beyond them.

*

Details of Markey's life help us respond to his work and see it in an art-historical context. A full biographical outline will not fit into this short essay; we have space only to look at aspects of his early life. He was born in 1918, the first child of David Marcus Robinson, a housepainter, and Hannah Hunt, a stitcher, of Arkwright Street, Belfast. Markey was named David Marcus after his father.

Where does this place Markey in the chronology of Irish painters? Taking northern painters as a frame of reference: by 1918, Paul Henry was 41, William Conor, 37 and Frank McKelvey, 23.

They were a different generation. Closer in age to Markey were Colin Middleton, Tom Carr and John Luke, they were his seniors by eight, nine and twelve years respectively. Next, his near contemporaries: Gerard Dillon was two years older; George Campbell, one year older; Dan O'Neill, two years younger; and Arthur Armstrong, six years younger. Then a gap opens up to Basil Blackshaw who was born in 1932.

Growing up in a relatively small city, Markey got to know many of these artists, particularly Dillon, Campbell, O'Neill and Armstrong. He also knew Conor, Middleton, Carr and Blackshaw, though less well. But Markey, always restless and constantly asserting his free spirit, was too individual to work closely with others or belong to a group.

Markey's great-grandfather, grandfather and father were involved in housepainting and paint contracting, and early in life he learned to mix commercial paints and the general tricks of the housepainting trade. Apart from occasionally helping his father, however, Markey was never a housepainter.

Formal education for Markey was limited to primary school at Perth Street Public Elementary School. Like many others of the time from a working-class background, he left school at fourteen. While at school his aptitude for drawing was recognised and to some extent encouraged. However, he received no systematic art training. He learned from art books and journals at the public library, briefly 'turned up' for some classes at the art college and worked for a short spell with the artist Sidney Smith who had a studio in Howard Street. In essence, Markey was self-taught, as were his contemporaries: Middleton, Dillon, O'Neill, Campbell and Armstrong. Dillon and O'Neill, both from working-class backgrounds, the former a housepainter and the latter an electrician, also learned from art books and journals.

Free of formal education, Markey entered a succession of jobs, moving from coach works to tram depot to motor works. His restlessness was already evident. By the time he was 19, he had started to journey abroad on merchant ships: an early trip took him to South America. Working at first as a 'pearl-diver' — a dish-washer/cook — on merchant ships and later as a steward on liners, he travelled to Canada, the US and Africa. Travel was a lifelong passion and it opened up his world. Up to his final years he made repeated private visits to France, Spain and North Africa. He regularly created for himself opportunities to travel to Paris, where he visited galleries and met other artists. For many others, such opportunities were open only on the basis of private income or public bursary.

At 20, Markey entered the Belfast shipyard to serve a five-year apprenticeship as a ship-welder. He started off on a weekly wage of six shillings with prospects of fifteen shillings by the fifth year. He did not like the yard and particularly disliked the fumes from welding. It was little surprise that he failed to complete his apprenticeship, thereby forfeiting his deposit of £2.

By then he had other things to occupy him, for in addition to being an occasional seaman and aspiring artist he had become a boxer. Fighting mostly in the bantam and lightweight divisions under the name Boyo Marko, or sometimes Boy Markey, he attracted the attention of local sports journalists: he was a 'fast improving boy'. Markey fought at Billy Downey's Club and Sammy Graham's Club, which were housed in converted stables in Conlig Street, and also at Ma Copley's at the Chapel Fields and the Rialto at the bottom of Peters Hill. By the time he was 25, Markey was losing interest in boxing. A local journalist captured the transition: 'As Boyo Marko, Robinson won many pots in the featherweight ring with a useful artistic left, but the palette had a stronger claim on him'.

On Christmas Day 1944, Markey married May Clarke. The marriage certificate describes him as an artist and her as a stitcher. The couple set up home in Lyle Street — now demolished due to urban re-development — just along the street from where his parents had moved in 1943. Later, the couple, with their two daughters Bernice and Annie, moved to nearby Queensland Street, located next to Tudor Place where the artist spent his final years.

In the 1940s and 1950s, an artist's life in Belfast, never easy, was particularly precarious. The late Arthur Armstrong once told me that between 1944 and 1953 he sold just one painting in Belfast and intimated how art seemed to be a furtive occupation at that time in Belfast.

But Markey was set on his course. Throughout the 1940s he exhibited regularly. In Belfast, he showed at the Ulster Academy of Art, later to become the Royal Ulster Academy; at the Civil Defence Arts and Crafts Exhibition, where his paintings of the April 1941 Belfast Blitz attracted much attention; and at Mills and Gray's Gallery. In Dublin, he showed at the inaugural Irish Exhibition of Living Art, the modernist salon set up in distinction to the more traditional academic strain in Irish art; and at the Country Tea Shop, then a popular exhibition space. In London, he exhibited at Heals Mansard Gallery and received mention in *Cornhill Magazine, Free French Periodical, Parade* and *Tatler.* Other exhibitions were to come in quick succession in the 1950s and in subsequent decades, when he exhibited in galleries such as the Oriel in Dublin and the Emer in Belfast.

By the end of the 1940s, Markey was being accepted as an artist, essentially on his own terms. Nomadic, mercurial, edgy and unpredictable, he was already a Belfast 'character'. The former welder and boxer, and sometime seaman, was moving in artistic circles. John Hewitt encouraged Markey and introduced him to other artists. Hewitt was not only a distinguished poet, but also an art assistant at the Belfast Museum and Art Gallery, and a founder member of CEMA, the Council for the Encouragement of Music and the Arts, later the Arts Council of Northern Ireland. Poets and painters alike were welcome at Hewitt's house at 18 Mount Charles. There, poets such as W. R. Rodgers and Roy McFadden mixed with painters such as Alicia Boyle, John Luke, Colin Middleton, Paul Nietsche, Rowell Friers and Markey. In conversation in 1995, Roy McFadden recalled for me how Markey referred to him and his associates as 'poets brooding in corners'.

Hewitt had some regard for Markey's work. In George and Arthur Campbell's book *Now in Ulster,* published in 1944, Hewitt wrote that any survey of contemporary artists under 40 would have to include Markey, who he described as 'a surprisingly subtle colourist'. Markey, though, grew disdainful of Hewitt. He produced a portrait of Hewitt and his wife Roberta in which she was appreciably the taller of the two, though in reality she was smaller, a physical distortion which captured a sense of her power in the relationship.

Markey had other, more exotic, associates including a Hungarian, a Ukrainian and an Englishman.

The Hungarian was Zoltan Lewinter-Frankl, a Jew, who fled Vienna in 1937, abandoning his clothing business. With his wife Anny he was bound for Australia via London. In London he was met by officials from Belfast and invited to visit Northern Ireland to explore the possibility of establishing a clothing business. After a well-orchestrated tour of some of the most affluent areas, the Frankls agreed to stay. They settled in Belfast and set up a successful knitwear factory in Newtownards — an early example of an Irish specialty: industrialisation by invitation.

Zoltan Frankl became an important figure in the arts: soon he was on the art advisory committee of CEMA and his home on the Malone Road was open to artists. His art collection was legendary: Stanley Spencer, Ivon Hitchers, Topolski, Epstein, Yeats, Conor, O'Neill and, of course, Markey. Frankl thought highly of Markey; in the foreword to the catalogue of one of Markey's most important exhibitions in the 1950s he wrote 'Markey Robinson is the most amazing personality I have met for some time'.

The Ukrainian was Paul Nietsche. From Kiev, but of German family, he travelled to Germany and England before arriving in Northern Ireland in the 1920s. Later, he was to be interned on the Isle of Man during World War II. Nietsche was an accomplished artist and had trained in Munich and Paris. Some 30 years older than Markey, he adopted the younger artist, helping him develop his technique and introducing him to Zoltan Frankl. Nietsche referred to Markey as 'a neglected genius'.

The Englishman was F. L. Green, known as Laurie Green.

Born in Portsmouth, he spent many years drifting around the south coast of England taking casual work in hotels, theatres, breweries, engineering works and shipyards. He came to Northern Ireland in the 1930s, settled there for almost twenty years and became a successful novelist. While there he befriended Frankl, Nietsche and Markey.

Green modelled his writing on Zola and Dostoevsky; he used Belfast as a setting and described real life characters. His most famous novel is *Odd Man Out,* published in 1945, and in it one of the real life characters is Markey. *Odd Man Out* is reminiscent of O'Flaherty's *The Informer.* It evokes some of the atmosphere of *Crime and Punishment,* but is excessively melodramatic. The plot revolves around a manhunt: Johnny Murtah, a terrorist, leads a failed robbery attempt on a mill during which he kills a cashier and is himself seriously wounded. On the run in Belfast, Murtah has various encounters. One of these is with an artist, Lukey Mulquin, who takes him to his studio and paints a portrait of the semi-conscious gunman.

Lukey is modelled on Markey. The names are similar, though perhaps Green was also conscious of the artist John Luke. Lukey and Markey sound like childish intonations of two of the evangelists. Their ages are similar: Lukey was 28 and Markey was 27 when the book was published. There are differences too: Lukey was an orphan at 15, Markey's parents were still alive and some of the dialogue involving Lukey is uncharacteristic of Markey. Overall, though, we can be in little doubt that the 'eccentric young artist' is Markey. Likewise, we can be sure that the character called Griffin is John Hewitt. In the book, Griffin recognises Lukey's 'genius' and encourages him. Talk of Dostoevsky and real life characterisation would have cut little ice with Markey; he was unhappy at his unwilling role in the book and for a short period was in dispute with Green.

Odd Man Out was made into an important film. Directed by Carol Reed and starring James Mason as Johnny Murtah, it was released in 1947 and has been described as 'a doomsday film noir'. The character of Lukey was played by Robert Newton and the portrait scene was something of a 'coup de cinema' for the time. The association with Markey stuck and was referred to in press coverage of some of his exhibitions at that time.

The image of Markey that emerges from the 1940s and 1950s, still early in his career, is that of a self-made painter connected with, though never assimilated into, the art world of Belfast and beginning to reach beyond it. Known to different generations of artists, encouraged by established figures in the arts community, a familiar figure among the fraternity of artists that met at Campbell's Café, he was part of the scene. In later decades, however, he was to recede into the background.

*

Markey Robinson was a prolific and multi-faceted artist. Best known for his landscapes, his paintings of gable-ends became something of a signature style. But there was more to Markey. He painted country, village and urban scenes; boats and fishing scenes; Spanish, French, African and Canadian scenes; Paris; the human figure — portraits, nudes, bathers, boxers, wrestlers, clowns; beach scenes; churches and religious scenes; circus scenes and 'scènes de ballet'; interiors — still life, table tops, windows opening on the sea; war scenes; wildlife; gypsy encampments; abstracts. The list goes on: there are many fugitive pieces and there is a vast unseen oeuvre. He also carved and sculpted: country folk, clowns, nudes, birds; he made model sailing ships and architectural models. The task of compiling a catalogue raisonné would be nightmarish.

He used whatever came to hand: driftwood, tree stumps, garden posts, stone. He seemed to cover every imaginable surface: panel, cardboard, paper, plasterboard, wallpaper, lino, lamp-shades, even glass; seldom canvas. Mostly these were materials that people discarded. Markey was quite happy to take them out of skips. He seldom painted with conventional oils, gouaches or acrylics. Instead, he often used commercial house paint, 'action' paint or 'pans' of poster paint.

It is astonishing that people still characterise Markey as a painter of gable-ends. This is, in part, testimony to the power of these works. They are a re-imagining of the Irish landscape, deliberately anachronistic, emphasising their own artificiality. They explore the essence of form; at times cubistic, at times almost abstract, they are antithetical to the 'cutesy' cottage scapes that proliferate in genteel Irish painting. This is new expressive terrain, a stylised world with huddles of cottages, belts of trees, menacing hills and simple statements of the human figure, solitary or in small groups, mostly women, their backs to the viewer. In some, the atmosphere is light and Markey plays with the geometry of gables and the language of flat shapes. In others, there is a brooding intensity, a Celtic gloom; man is subordinate to nature. And the Irish landscape, stripped to stark simplicity, is moved into a psychological field. This is too knowing to be primitive; it is expressionist. But why worry about labels: here is good old-fashioned modern painting.

Did Markey paint too much? No doubt he painted his share of potboilers. He destroyed little and kept nothing for himself. That was his way. He produced cascades of work, but though he was quick he was never slaphappy. Many of the major figures in art history had the same enviable facility; we are told that Monet produced *Impression: Sunrise* in less than an hour.

The important point is that in his work Markey maintained his creative vitality. His ability to constantly innovate adds to the stature of the work. Working prolifically, he gained freedom in composition and improvisational mastery; some pictures executed at speed are as spontaneous as a summer breeze.

But it is not only critics who are entitled to judge whether an artist produced too much; the market also has a say. Here the evidence is reasonably clear: Markey's work is in demand and prices have risen.

For someone like Markey Robinson, who led an eventful life and produced a huge volume of work, there can be no last word. One can recount the life and examine the work and, somewhere between anecdote and analysis, try to convey a sense of the man and his achievement. Certain things are sure, he was one of the channels whereby 'modern' art belatedly entered into the insular Ireland of the 1930s, 1940s and 1950s, but more than that, he was an important painter and a creative maverick.

'MARKEY'
by Peter Knuttel

'MARKEY

Portraits of Markey Robinson

*Markey Robinson at his exhibition in the Country Tea Shop,
Dublin, 1952*

*Markey Robinson with Arthur Campbell at an exhibition of works by
George and Arthur Campbell in the Mol Gallery, Belfast, 1943*

 **Michael D. Higgins**

My Mother Married my Father in Mount Melleray in 1937

My mother married my father in Mount Melleray
in 1937

Those photos were the most precious
From before.
She in slight profile
Her best side
He fresh and determined
A strong face they said.
She wore her leather coat
For the going away
And he a blue grey jacket
In its lapel a badge
Given as a gift
Among many blessings
By the monk who performed their ceremony.

My mother married my father in Mount Melleray
in 1937

Why should we not weep
And make the salt
For others' tears
That teach to grieve
And source the long sigh
That breaks
Out of breath shaken
From the spirit
That trembles in its search
For truth.

My mother married my father in Mount Melleray
in 1937

The remembered humiliation
The humiliation of another's loss
Suggests a press of tears
That is too far from the heart
Distant from the source
That might connect the long sigh

To the wound deep
In interrupted breath
I weep for the lost child
Not allowed by times
Made adult too soon
To gaze at joy exchanged
Hear words bartered
In laughter.
It is the little things
That make a resonance
For certain
In oblique constancy
Lodged in creviced memory
They hold on
And blossom.

*My mother married my father in Mount Melleray
in 1937*

On the side of a stony mill
My father
Going away again
An exotic visitor
Tells me he will walk the remaining mile along
To a bus that will pause in front of the familiar
Withering cabbage plants in bundles
Fork and rakes in pristine cleanliness.
As we turned from each other
I place my frail hope
In his surviving energy
From the warmth of his jacket lapel
He takes a badge
Worn since his marriage.

*My mother married my father in Mount Melleray
in 1937*

It is an old indented badge
Moulded for the finishing through
And the anchoring
Not temporary
Image enamelled
Of a cross a hand
With reds and greens I cannot now distribute
Sign of a confraternity

A special membership
Something stubborn
Intimate
That had migrated with him
In his despair
From lapel of once sturdy jacket
In fashion
Chosen for discretion in celebration
To the familiar coat
Of frayed intimacies
Now worn
For warmth in the necessity
Of his visit
To us children
That he had already half lost
Its leathered cuffs asserting
A dignity of craft
Perhaps a prudence.

*My mother married my father in Mount Melleray
in 1937*

No coins left
Nothing to give
He takes it from his coat
The badge more precious
Upon which my eyes had feasted
In his proximity.
He offers this gift in a hand I never kissed.
I kept it with me.
And lost it in my own migrations.
When I remember now
This sacred little thing
I want to grieve for him
And let his anger go
And my childish shame.

*My mother married my father in Mount Melleray
in 1937*

I keep this secret gift
For my father
In the space shared
Between us.
In a world of shortening time

Why is it not allowed to remember
Why is it required to abuse
Small and sacred moments
Scarce and precious things
From the spaces of between
In iceberg times
Of forbidden touch
The slightest sign of tears
And love.

My mother married my father in Mount Melleray
in 1937

Ever through grief
The healing is uncertain
For all belief is thin belief
But little things can lodge
On a fragile surface
Create a boundless aura
That enables the memory
To make a miracle.

My mother married my father in Mount Melleray
in 1937

Eve Patten

The Backward Look: History and the New Irish Fiction

In *The International* (1999), Glenn Patterson takes as his subject a key moment in modern Irish history — the weekend in which the Northern Ireland Civil Rights Association was inaugurated in Belfast in 1967. Ironically, however, the political material of the novel is out of focus, as the author shifts attention from this 'historic' event to the micronarratives in which it was embedded. The account of the International, the Belfast hotel in which the first significant meeting of the Association took place, is constructed from the contingent and disparate stories of its occupants: the guests, waitresses and barmen whose lives are momentarily illuminated in the shadow of history. Simultaneously, the narrative technique substitutes fragmentation for continuity, highlighting the interruption of conversations and journeys, the frustrations of half-formed relationships, the constant breaks in the flow of an ordinary evening in the hotel. The result is a narrative splintered into individual biographies, with little sense of coherence or objectivity. *The International* is about the rupturing of 'history' by historical reality, and the refusal of the past to be constrained by the teleological pull of the present.

Patterson's novel has appeared at the end of a decade of Irish fiction dominated by history. Like several other Irish writers — John Banville in *The Book of Evidence* (1989), Eugene McCabe in *Death and Nightingales* (1992), and Carlo Gebler in *How to Murder a Man* (1998) — his interest as a writer is in the ambiguities and subjectivities that are, in effect, written out of our contemporary versions of the past. For each of these novelists, fiction has provided an opportunity to reconstruct an aspect of Irish history that reveals its essential recalcitrance to the dominant narratives of the present, its deeply problematic lack of cohesion and linearity. Like contemporary British fiction, which, in recent years, has carried out a rigorous critical engagement with the defining narratives of Englishness — the 'victory' of World War I or the legacy of Thatcherism, the Irish novel has been concerned with destabilising readings of the past that offer any kind of complacency or national consensus.[1]

In critical terms, this trajectory of Irish prose has provided narratives that the critic Steven Connor, discussing the British novel and history, describes as 'transformative'. Their function is to 'criticise, displace, limit, interrupt' existing historiographies, and their effect is to disturb not only established, even clichéd, accounts, but also the mechanics through which events and lives are rendered as 'history' in the first place. Despite its obvious postmodern affiliations, this kind of writing has not gained as much attention in Ireland as what Connor identifies as the more traditional novel of 'cultural enlargement'. Here, the past is aligned according to the needs of a contemporary agenda, serving to consolidate rather than undermine identity. 'In the case of historical narrative', he suggests, 'this effect of binding consolidation works in a collective as well as an individual way. To narrate a history is often both to imagine collectively and to imagine a collectivity'.[2] And arguably it is this second narrative tendency, which seeks to stabilise rather than deconstruct a public narrative of history, which has galvanised the distinctive writers of the so-called New Irish Fiction.

So cohesive is the grouping of Dermot Bolger, Roddy Doyle, Colm Tóibín and Joseph O'Connor that criticism has evolved a specific tag for them — these are the 'Robinsonian' novelists, whose emergence coincided with a period of *glasnost* in the Republic of Ireland following the appointment of Mary Robinson as president in 1990.[3] The ethos of revisionist self-analysis and post-national liberalisation that Robinson helped to foster has been seen as intrinsic to the way in which these novelists have responded to the accelerated process of change in Ireland since the 1950s and 1960s, decades in which most of them were born or grew up. The predominant trajectory of their work is, as a result, historical in a specific and reflexive sense. Characteristically, their fiction implicitly or overtly links the damaged social and political landscape of the Irish present — a 'Celtic Tiger' culture split between smug financial self-interest and grievous social breakdown — to misdirections in the past, and the cataclysmic dysfunctionalism of family, church and state in the mid-twentieth century.

The New Irish Fiction has taken responsibility, therefore, for the indictment of a previous generation, and the identification of its abuses and failings as the root cause of contemporary disaffection. In particular, these writers have targeted the post-independence legacy of moral repression identified with the terms of the 1937 Constitution and the protectionist policies of Eamon de Valera's government. Ireland's gradual emergence from a de Valerian ideology, the difficult transition from rural to urban, Catholic to secular, insular republicanism to European cosmopolitanism, has frequently been narrativised as an Oedipal struggle or the rebellion of a disturbed adolescent against a debilitating and corrupt patriarchy. Fictional critique has thus been focused on the inadequacy of the father-figures embedded in the chain of paternalistic authority in Irish life — the priest, the legislator, the politician — as part of a revitalised engagement with the classic father/son trope of modern literature. In this respect, the struggle between past and present is identified primarily in masculine terms, a factor that has undoubtedly helped to sustain the predominance of male writers in the contemporary literary scene in Ireland.[4]

The novel frequently taken as the defining voice of the new generation is Dermot Bolger's *The Journey Home* (1990). In this work, Bolger's transition between past and present sets up a contrast between the complacency of an older generation, deracinated from rural life but settled in a suburban interzone, and the alienation of a younger generation for whom 'home' is the uneasy landscape of an inner city racked with drug abuse, exploitation, flitting sexual gratification and poverty. When his own father dies, the protagonist, Hano, can find no alternative parentage in the institutional authorities of the country. The focus for his anger is a politician, Patrick Plunkett, who embodies the corruption endemic to the Irish state. Manipulative and deceitful, Plunkett's travesty of Irish moral values and of the family itself is indicated by his coprophiliac sexual perversion. Ironically, he and his businessman brother bear the surname of one of the heroes of the 1916 Easter Rising, but the Plunkett family clearly represents the betrayal of Ireland's heroic idealism and the ultimate victory of opportunism, extortion and sleaze. Bolger's intense, nightmarish vision of contemporary Irish society is, it is implied, the logical outcome of the ascendancy of a warped and mercenary version of paternalism. The meandering journey of the two central characters, on the run from the police as the novel opens, symbolises the detachment of a young Ireland that lacks the security of national identity and community tradition.

With its focus on the dystopianism of Ireland's capital city, *The Journey Home* engages the civic perspective of a generation of novelists still troubled by the country's gravitational shift from rural integration to urban alienation. In its particular use of the metaphor of the family — a nostalgic idealism clashing with a vicious reality — it shares in contemporary fiction's broad preoccupation with the unravelling of constitutional mythologies. The enshrinement of the family as central to the collaborative operations of church and state in the 1937 Constitution, Article 41.1.1° of which recognises and pledges the protection of the family unit as 'a moral institution possessing inalienable and imprescriptable rights', provides the ironic backdrop to novels which repeatedly acknowledge a social landscape of marital breakdown, sexual repression and physical abuse. Roddy Doyle's *Paddy Clarke, Ha Ha Ha* (1993), for example, looks back to the late 1960s, and the distress of a young boy experiencing the failure of his parent's marriage within the unsympathetic climate of a deeply conservative Irish Catholicism. Patrick McCabe's black comedy *The Butcher Boy* (1992) sets the tragic collapse of a highly dysfunctional family in the highly dysfunctional community of small-town Ireland in the 1960s, and even portrays the sexual molestation of the disturbed adolescent protagonist by a reform-school priest as a parodic distortion of 'normal' family relations between father and son, husband and wife.

The novel in which the inadequacy of Ireland's Constitution is most systematically explored is Colm Tóibín's *The Heather Blazing* (1992). This novel seeks to highlight the extent of the ideological gulf between the priorities of a bygone Ireland immersed in the legacy of the struggle for independence, and the needs of a present-day state, which must be responsible for the welfare of its citizens. Eamon Redmond, the novel's protagonist, has been named after Eamon de Valera, and his route to a position as High Court judge is fuelled by a Fianna Fáil political organisation entrenched in the values of nationalism, Catholicism and the Constitution. Now the viability of that ethos is at issue. For Redmond, the attempt to find continuity between his childhood in County Wexford and his adult professional life in the capital is increasingly difficult, as the principles of his father's generation repeatedly clash with the changed priorities of modern Dublin. The ideological fracture comes into focus when a particular legal case is brought before him in court: a sixteen-year-old girl has become pregnant and is challenging the decision of her school to expel her. As Redmond works to arrive at a judgment, he re-reads Article 41 of the Constitution, and attempts to make sense of its terminology:

> What was a family? The Constitution did not define a family, and at the time it was written in 1937 the term was perfectly understood: a man, his wife and their children. But the Constitution was written in the present tense, it was not his job to decide what certain terms — he wrote 'certain terms' in his note-pad, underlined it and wrote 'uncertain terms' below that — such as 'the family' had meant in the past. It was his job to define and redefine those terms now. Could not a girl and her child be a family? And if they were did the girl have rights arising from her becoming a mother, thus creating a family, greater than the rights of any institution?[5]

Redmond eventually decides in favour of the school, which not only conflicts with the prevailing mood of a young society, but, worse, hypocritically disguises his own family situation, for he has already become the grandfather of a child born outside marriage. His intransigence can be no more than a temporary stopgap, however, against the processes of social change, which Tóibín, in his chosen metaphor of a crumbling western coastline, suggests to be both natural and inevitable, the gradual erosion of Ireland's former contours providing for the emergence of a whole new landscape.

The interventionist nature of this retrospective voice in the New Irish Fiction inevitably gained its authors a certain profile, but it also exposed them to critical scepticism on several fronts. First, there was the sense that their use of Ireland, both past and present, was strategic to the point of becoming opportunist. Declan Kiberd perceived a disingenuousness in the newer novelists, who wrote of a disillusioned and impoverished society while reaping the benefits of economic and cultural resurgence. 'Bolger's posture of radical dissent came rather oddly', he has written, 'from one who throughout the period was feted by the *Irish Times* and accorded a seat on the Arts Council'.[6] For many readers, the gap between author and subject was heavily ironic, with the writers in question seen as assuming an outdated role — that of the heavily censored and peripheralised Irish artist of the 1950s — when in reality, they were intrinsic to the liberal cosmopolitanism and commercially-driven consensus of Ireland in the 1990s.

Second, and despite its claim to be the cutting-edge, the New Irish Fiction has been far from radical, far from 'new'. Stylistically, and with the exception of Patrick McCabe's surrealist *Gothic*, it has foregrounded a fairly conservative social realism as the appropriate form for the interrogation of Irish inequities and hypocrisies. This has no doubt been at the critical expense of those novels, such as Mary Morrissey's allegorical *Mother of Pearl* (1996), which took risks with metafictional experimentation. When combined with their heavily sociological emphasis on 'the matter of Ireland', it has also meant that the New Irish Fiction writers are liable to come across as distinctly 'old school', updated versions of the defiantly realist prose writers of the counter-revival in the 1940s and 1950s. For Sean O'Faolain's generation, the literary agenda was clear: write about reality, rather than the 'Ireland' which the poets had imagined, in order to undercut the mythology shaped so influentially by Yeats and the revival. In the first editorial of the literary journal *The Bell*, in 1940, O'Faolain urged his colleagues towards life, rather than art. 'Write about your gateway, your well-field, your street corner, your girl, your boatslip, pubs, books, pictures, dogs, horses, river, tractor, anything at all that has a hold on you.'[7] While current productivity might be packaged as a renaissance, it represents at the same time a continuation of this agenda, with its would-be oppositional, secularising and anthropological instincts, in homage to John McGahern more than, say, Flann O'Brien.

Indeed, as Gerry Smyth has illustrated, a limited and formulaic Irish realism has become the necessary mode for any Irish writer wishing to publish in England, a point which brings into focus the many problems that surround the determining relationship between the New Irish Fiction and an international readership.[8] There is certainly a danger that the success of the contemporary Irish novel (and, increasingly, screenplay) within a British and American market has fostered a creative determinism, clamping down on variation. Elsewhere, Smyth has commented on the reflex of the younger generation of novelists who, having successfully exported a particular version of Ireland to the world, have paradoxically returned to a narrowness of vision and a cultural insularity in terms of their understanding of home. 'So assured has the new generation become of the inherent interest of novelistic representations of Ireland and Irishness', he suggests, 'that there appears to be little impetus to look beyond the Irish experience at what is happening in other cultures'.[9] A lack of perspective or a self-obsessiveness fuelled by contemporary Irish fiction's international momentum thus emerges as a potential straitjacket on creativity and expansion.

Perhaps expectations of what Irish fiction *should* be are already carving out a shortcut to stagnation. The images prioritised by the New Irish Fiction, described by Kiberd as 'the conceptual clichés of a strangely caricatured Dublin landscape of horses in high-rise flats and doomed young things in squalid bedsits', have evolved a fossilised mythology.[10] What one audience has appreciated as the radical tragi-comedy of 'northside realism' has been dismissed by the critic Shaun Richards as a dangerous lapse into a new Celtic twilight, damagingly stereotypical in the way it functions for a non-Irish readership as representative of Ireland as a whole.[11] In similar terms, the academic Desmond Fennell has accused contemporary writers such as Roddy Doyle, Frank McCourt and Patrick McCabe of projecting an Ireland that is essentialist, whimsical and distinctly provincial, in writing which is valued 'for its occasional strong depiction of a life that is subadult, subliterate, offbeat, weird, poor, and possessed of a naive, occasionally hilarious charm', but not for the depth of its philosophical engagement with life in general.[12]

Therefore the New Irish Fiction's success has not gone unchallenged, particularly as the many shared concerns of the younger generation of novelists have encouraged a critical reductivism, the tarring of all with the same sceptical brush. In fact, there are significant differences of style and subject matter between, say Dermot Bolger and Colm Tóibín, or between Roddy Doyle and Patrick McCabe. The ease of the Robinsonian tag creates an illusion of homogeneity that quickly gives way to a reality of thematic variety, including, from Tóibín in particular, a distinctly European self-awareness.[13] Nonetheless, the profile of this group of writers does raise questions about how fiction has been used in Ireland in the 1990s. Has the 'confessional and anthropological ethos' of the novel as social document been at the cost, as Gerry Smyth has suggested, of intellectual speculation and technique?[14] Have the images of Ireland evolved by these writers crossed the line from authenticity into caricature? And most important perhaps, has their use of the 'backward look' according to the demands of a contemporary postcolonial agenda compromised their response to the complexity of history as a process?

It is the latter question that ultimately defines the New Irish Fiction, and demarcates it from the alternative novelistic trajectory described at the beginning of this essay. The constraining of the past to the present by contemporary writers has inevitably raised a critical backlash. It has been suggested, for example, that the version of Ireland they collectively endorse is less than accurate: an exaggeration of past abuses and present dissatisfactions. Declan Kiberd has identified in the writing of Bolger and his colleagues a tendency to sentimentalise the victimisation of a younger generation by a tyrannical, corrupt and priest-ridden order, in representations which largely ignore the already well-established retreat of Catholicism as the dominant ideology in Irish society.[15] In the same vein, the privileging of a recent past — southern Irish society from the mid-twentieth century to the present — combined with the imposition of an implicitly causal narrative, has functioned to blur history with parable, evolving a lapsarian mythology documenting the transition from independence to contemporary disaffection as a fall from grace. This is the past as shaped from the moral high ground of the present, and organised with the full benefit of fin-de-siècle hindsight. The 'story' which predominates, establishes today's damaged society as the inevitable outcome of yesterday's belated independence and traumatised path to nationhood.

The overall effect is a school of fiction that endorses, on behalf of the reading community, a particular narrative of the nation, a twentieth-century saga of postcolonial disaffection, villainy and blame. The retrospective stance of the New Irish Fiction provides a cohesive, collective version of history, which tends to override intractability or ambiguity in favour of a simple, linear consensus; just as the high profile of the Robinsonian novelists has obscured the complexity and deconstructive impulse of Irish writers whose versions of the past are less topical and ultimately more ambiguous. While this does not detract from the attractiveness of their work to its immediate audience, nor from their relevance to contemporary ideological transitions, it may well place a time limit on their centrality to the preoccupations of contemporary literary culture in Ireland. It is this factor, finally, which really ties the New Irish Fiction down to its era, grounding both the nature and purpose of its predominant 'backward look' to the particular socio-political concerns of the 1990s, and to an engagement with history which is perhaps more journalistic than philosophical.

Notes

1   British historical fiction in the same period has ranged from the highly disruptive readings of the Great War in Pat Barker's *Regeneration Trilogy* (1991–5) to numerous political satires on post-war Britain and Thatcherism, including Margaret Drabble's *The Radiant Way* (1989), Michael Dibdin's *Dirty Tricks* (1991) and Jonathan Coe's *What a Carve Up!* (1994). See D. J. Taylor, *After the War: The Novel and England since 1945* (London: Chatto, 1993), chapter 12.

2   Steven Connor, *The English Novel in History: 1950–1995* (London: Routledge, 1996), pp. 4–5.

3   The term 'New Irish Fiction' was in regular usage before it was academically cemented by Gerry Smyth, who also evolved the 'Robinsonian' label. I am indebted to his useful book *The Novel and the Nation: Studies in the New Irish Fiction* (London: Pluto, 1997).

4   Several critics have explored the predominance of the father/son relationship in Irish writing. See, for example, Edna Longley, 'When Did You Last See Your Father?', in *The Living Stream: Literature and Revisionism in Ireland* (Newcastle: Bloodaxe, 1994), and Declan Kiberd, 'Fathers and Sons', in *Inventing Ireland: The Literature of the Modern Nation* (1995; London: Vintage, 1996).

5   Colm Tóibín, *The Heather Blazing* (London: Pan, 1992), p. 90.

6   Kiberd, *Inventing Ireland*, p. 609.

7   Editorial, *The Bell*, vol. 1, no. 1 (October 1940), p. 7.

8   Gerry Smyth, 'Being Difficult: The Irish Writer in Britain', *Éire-Ireland*, vol. 31, no. 3 (Fall/Winter 1996), pp. 41–57.

9   Smyth, *The Novel and the Nation*, p. 177.

10 Kiberd, *Inventing Ireland*, p. 609.

11 Shaun Richards, 'Northside Realism and the Twilight's Last Gleaming', *Irish Studies Review*, no. 2 (Winter 1992), pp. 18–20.

12 Desmond Fennell, 'A Provincial Passion: Cleansing Irish Literature of Irishness', *Éire-Ireland*, vol. 32, no. 3 (Summer/Fall 1997), p. 198.

13 I am thinking, for example, of Tóibín's 1990 novel, *The South*, which juxtaposes mid-twentieth century Ireland with Spain in the wake of the civil war.

14 Smyth, *The Novel and the Nation*, p. 177.

15 Kiberd, *Inventing Ireland*, p. 609.

 Fintan O'Toole

Culture and Conflict

There is a word in many European languages for the worst kind of narrow-minded loyalty to your own side — chauvinism. It conjures up the flag-waving patriot who supports his country right or wrong; the swaggering tribalist who believes in the innate superiority of his own identity; the pig-headed man who belittles women. It is widely believed that the term comes from a famous French warrior-patriot, Nicholas Chauvin, whose exploits in the Napoleonic wars made him the living image of extreme and belligerent nationalism. And indeed it does: there was a Nicholas Chauvin and he did display all of those attitudes. But Chauvin was not a real man. He was an artistic creation. He was invented for the mid-nineteenth-century French stage. He figures in Scribe's *Le Soldat Laboreur*, Cogniard's *La Cocarde Tricolore*, Bayard and Dumanoir's *Les Aides-de-Camp*, and Charet's *Conscrit Chauvin*. He is a peasant who retires to his smallholding after the wars, but who keeps his musket oiled and his uniform hung with medals near at hand. He tells the village boys lurid tales of how he slaughtered the foreigners. While ploughing in his fields, he regularly turns up the bones of those who have died for 'la patrie' in the past. The myths of blood and soil are all around him.

These days, when we tend to think of art and culture as the opposite of violence and narrow-mindedness, it is well to remember that Chauvin is the creation of writers. For chauvinism, and the conflict it engenders, is often rooted in the very things that artists work with: a sense of belonging, an awareness of tradition, an attempt to create powerful and emotive images of the life of a people. And 'culture', that broad but pervasive set of assumptions, values and meanings to which all art relates, has a far more ambivalent relationship to conflict than we often expect.

If the twentieth century taught us anything, it is that culture is no defence against barbarism. In the middle of the nineteenth century, the English poet and critic Matthew Arnold wrote a book called *Culture and Anarchy*, the very title implying that culture is the alternative to chaos and conflict. Culture, to him, was the opposite of 'bitter envying and strife': 'culture hates hatred; culture has one great passion, the passion for sweetness and light'. But in our times sweetness and light are not the most obvious qualities of culture. It is not just that the creative people are ultimately powerless against guns and prison camps or that the cultured person is at the mercy of the ignorant killer. It is something much worse: the cultured person and the ignorant killer have often been one and the same. Intellectuals and artists have sometimes taken the lead in violent conflicts. Their brilliance has been used to create hateful propaganda. Their rhetoric has fuelled destructive passions. Their exaggerated attachment to their own culture has fed a sense of superiority that can only be assuaged by domination.

The twentieth century's most ferocious and single-minded act of irrational violence — the Nazi extermination of the Jews — came about, not in some uncivilised backwater, but at the heart of 'cultured' Europe. As George Steiner (1979) has put it:

> Not only did the general dissemination of literary, cultural values prove no barrier to totalitarianism; but in notable instances the high places of humanistic learning and art actually welcomed and aided the new terror. Barbarism prevailed on the very ground of Christian humanism, of renaissance culture and classic rationalism. We know that some of the men who devised and administered Auschwitz had been trained to read Shakespeare or Goethe, and continued to do so.

Likewise, in the terrible collapse of Yugoslavia in the 1990s and its consequences in murderous conflict, artists sometimes fed fantasies of national pride, of a mythic cultural greatness that had been shamed and that must be re-asserted. In the development of aggressive Serbian nationalism, for example, the key document, published in 1989, was a memorandum, drawn up under the direction of the distinguished novelist Dobrica Cosic, claiming that the Serbs were a persecuted nation and proposing that 'the integrity of the Serb people' be the major aim of all future policy. Cosic's document, the work of a cultured artist, has, in the words of the historian Noel Malcolm (1998), 'been seen in retrospect as a virtual manifesto for the 'Greater Serbian' policies pursued by Belgrade in the 1990s'.

There is indeed, at the deepest level, a close connection between the artistic imagination and the nationalist impulse. Nations, as we know, are not the products of nature or of biology. They are not really the expression of blood and soil. They are cultural constructs, emerging, just as surely as a novel or a play or a photograph does, from the intersection of a given historical reality and the imagination, of memories and desires. And precisely because they are invented, they are always open to the possibility of being imagined differently. That possibility is, for many, too disturbing to contemplate. It leaves too much open, allows for too much uncertainty. So there is always a strong temptation to forget or deny the act of invention and to pretend that the nation is eternal, that its truth is contained in the glorious past and that the main task of artists and cultural institutions is to preserve the purity of a timeless, immemorial impulse by cutting away, either metaphorically or, in extreme cases, literally, those who are impure.

For artists, there is a particular temptation to pretend that what they are doing in the here-and-now is merely a revival of something old and authentic that has been buried by inauthentic, foreign elements that have crept in from the outside. Artists are, and must be, acutely aware of tradition, of the long history of the forms they use. Connecting your own work with some allegedly timeless tradition gives it, moreover, a dignity and a status that seem all the more important when an artist comes from a culture that has been oppressed or marginalised or abused. The act of reclamation, or re-asserting the value of a lost or suppressed culture, can be immensely liberating, releasing a trapped energy and making articulate voices that had been silenced.

But it can all too easily become a dangerous lie. It is a short step from asserting the value of a culture to claiming for it a special superiority. The very process of defining, for example Irish or Serb or Iranian culture, too often begins with the word not. The real Irish culture is whatever is not English. The authentic Serb culture is, above all, not Islamic. The genuine Iranian culture is that which is purged of all things that are not Islamic. Whatever is the opposite of them must, by a process of elimination, be us. And, under pressure, that process of elimination can become all too literal. By denying the priority of the present over the past, by insisting that there is or ever can be such a thing as a pure culture, the search for authenticity that underpins nationalism can also underpin the most terrible atrocities.

One thing we have to remember is that culture is not just about our collective images of ourselves. It is also about our collective images of others. And those inherited images may be utterly destructive. Just because a habit of mind is authentic, does not mean that it is good. Prejudices, hatreds, patronising generalisations, false assumptions and contemptuous attitudes may be deeply rooted, venerable, time-honoured and steeped in tradition. Conversely, toleration, respect, a willingness to embrace diversity, and sympathy for people unlike ourselves, may be the products of very recent experience. Bad habits may be, in a narrow sense, a much more authentic expression of a culture than good ones.

And, of course, what is true of our images of other cultures is just as true of a culture's images of out-groups within the nation itself. We like to think of culture as a generous, all-embracing, inclusive concept. It can be all of those things, but it is also, inevitably, about power. The power to define a culture also contains the power to define who is not really part of it. To describe someone as uncultured is to imply that he or she is inhuman, unworthy of the rights of a citizen. And the easiest way to become uncultured is to be ignored by cultural institutions. Simply by painting them out of the picture and writing them out of the story, the poor, immigrants, gypsies, political dissidents, gay men and lesbians, social non-conformists can be rendered at best invisible, at worst intolerable. That in itself creates two of the preconditions for conflict: prejudice on the one side and alienation on the other.

Yet we still tend to think of culture as a force for peace and stability. One of the most wrong-headed assumptions of the late twentieth century was that there is a direct relationship between cultural unity on the one side and social and political equilibrium on the other. Looking at the awful fate of the former Yugoslavia in the 1990s, we are tempted to conclude that the violence and hatred expressed there are an almost inevitable result of the presence of so many different cultures within too small a space. If the Bosnians, Serbs, Croatians and Albanians were not so different, we think, they would be able to live together in peace and harmony. Difference creates conflict. Conversely, similarity fosters an attitude of co-operation and mutual sympathy. This notion seems to make obvious sense. Even in personal life, after all, we take it for granted that we can be most intimate, most relaxed, with a 'compatible' partner, with someone whose basic thoughts, feelings and instincts are the same as our own.

But what then of Cambodia or Rwanda? Here, for example, is Ben Kiernan's description of Cambodia in his book *The Pol Pot Regime*:

> It was geographically compact, demographically dispersed, linguistically unified, ethnically homogenous, socially undifferentiated, culturally uniform, administratively unitary, politically undeveloped, economically undiversified . . .

If cultural difference is at the root of conflict, Cambodia should have been a haven of tranquillity. It is landlocked and isolated. It had an elaborate traditional culture. Its people were to an overwhelming extent the same people: Khmer-speaking peasants. And yet it became, in the 1970s and 1980s, the scene of one of the worst campaigns of systematic extermination of the twentieth century, in which about 20 per cent of the population was wiped out.

The truth is that every culture, by its very nature, has within itself both a force for sympathy and solidarity and a force for hatred and conflict. Differences between peoples are not racial or biological, but cultural. They arise from a very definite process of experiences and encounters. They are cultural constructs, invented and re-invented to further particular ends at particular times. The two basic words in the formation of every culture are 'us' and 'them', and they are inextricably linked to each other. We define 'us' as 'not them'. We identify ourselves by way of contrast with others. The very process by which we come to see ourselves as part of a society and a community is also the process by which we begin to exclude others. The generosity and openness which make us feel responsible for members of our own culture may become, under stress, the bigotry and cruelty which make us feel that we have no responsibility to members of another culture.

Art shares this condition. The same epic poem about the medieval Battle of Kosovo Field that makes Serbs feel inextricably bound to one another may also encourage them to slaughter Albanians. The cinematic myths of the Wild West that helped to bind together the diverse immigrant cultures of America celebrated the virtual extermination of the Native Americans. Much of the great architecture that defines the public spaces of European and Asian cities was built with the spoils of war, slavery and colonisation. Many of the most powerful images in the history of photography are images of war, impossible to imagine in the absence of the most appalling upheaval. Conflict has often been, in all the arts, a spur to creativity.

One of the big things that happened in the late twentieth century, moreover, was that the cultural sphere grew enormously. It used to be possible to think of culture as a relatively free space, at a distance from economics, politics and everyday social life. The freedom may have been somewhat illusory and the distance may have been much narrower than artists like to imagine, but both were nonetheless real. In the last few decades, however, there has been what Frederic Jameson (1991) describes as:

> . . . a prodigious expansion of culture throughout the social realm, to the point at which everything in our social life — from economic value and state power . . . to the very structure of the psyche itself — can be said to have become "cultural".

Think of the way that imagery has become central to economics, so that the value of, say, a pair of running shoes, has but a distant relationship to the materials and labour used to make it, and is mostly determined by the aura that has been created around it by the film-makers who made the ads, the writers who thought up the slogans and the stars who lent their glamour to it in return for vast sums of money. Think, too, of the centrality of the media to contemporary politics. Successful election campaigns are now run as self-conscious, dramatic narratives: scripted, costumed, designed and performed with the kind of deliberation that used to be reserved for the theatre.

Inevitably, as culture has become more central to the real world of power and money, it has itself become a battleground in the conflicts that power and money generate. Polite racists have shifted their ground of argument from the claims of race and biology to the claims of culture: since it is no longer acceptable to attack immigrant communities on the grounds of racial inferiority, they tend to attack them on the grounds of alleged cultural incompatibility. In reaction against the forces of globalisation, nativist movements rally to the defence of supposedly endangered cultures. In response to social and political upheavals, cynical leaders manipulate a sense of cultural distinctiveness to mobilise popular sentiment. Disagreements about the political and economic direction of society are re-imaged as 'culture wars', expressions not merely of competing interests but of fundamentally opposed mindsets.

How can artists and cultural institutions respond to these forces? One obvious response is to go on pretending that there is still a separate cultural space, removed from the mean world of social and political conflicts. Many artists and institutions instinctively fall back on Matthew Arnold's formulation of culture as the realm of sweetness and light that acts as a corrective to the bitter strife of everyday life. Many persist in the notion that art is implicitly and necessarily redemptive; that art always makes people better, more humane, more generous. But for anyone who is alive to the world in which we live, these comforting illusions are not an option.

Yet danger also lies in the opposite direction. Artists and institutions who engage with the reality of conflict can become implicated in the conflict itself. They can end up, consciously or unconsciously, as propagandists. They can fall for the allure of being the voice of the tribe, of dignifying squalid deeds with beautiful images.

Artists have, though, some built-in mechanisms for avoiding these dangers. One is the horror of clichés. The cultural constructs that are used to promote conflict are always saturated with clichés. They always depend on hollow caricatures and on hackneyed assumptions. They inflate minor differences into huge issues. They distort rich, complex and vibrant traditions into grotesque self-parodies.

But while clichés can make for successful politics, they can never make for successful art. In this sense, it does not matter greatly whether artists are good or bad people. If they are to be good artists, they are forced to make things new, to alter the angle of vision, to deal in complexities, ambiguities and contradictions. In doing so, they bear witness to the fact that reality itself is not as simple as the propagandist would have us believe. And they make fixed, pre-determined ideas potentially open and malleable.

Another powerful mechanism in art is its particularity. Where those who create conflict tend to deal in abstract generalisations, art has to deal with specifics. Even so-called abstract art has to be utterly precise in the way it uses its materials. Art exists in the details. And details inevitably tend to humanise the subject. The closer we get, the more clearly we see and recognise the familiar humanity in the face of the Other.

And there is, finally, the natural contrariness of art. The very decision to make art, particularly in a situation of conflict, is a perverse one. It goes against the grain. It is out of keeping with the times. And it often begins with the act of trying to imagine that the world is not the way it is. It tends to start with the question: 'what if?'; and that, of course, is the very question that those who have an interest in sustaining conflict do not want us to ask.

Artists do not, moreover, have to choose between isolation and non-involvement on the one side and participation and collaboration on the other. They can, if they are smart enough, find forms of engagement that do not involve collusion. They can identify with their 'own side' by holding the mirror up to its failings and absurdities. They can use traditional, accepted images, but subvert their approved meanings. They can find the contradictions within their own cultures and use them to open up what has been closed down. Sometimes, when they can do nothing else without being killed or tortured, they can make work that is so dense, so metaphorical, that its real meaning will become clear only after the dark times have passed. Then, at least someone in the future will be able to say that not everyone within that society went along with what was being done in their name. These may be small consolations, but there are times when humanity itself survives only in the seemingly insignificant details.

None of these qualities actually solve conflicts or deflect the injustice, bigotry and cynicism that cause them. But together they do constitute a set of resources that can be deployed, especially in the wake of conflict. Artists and cultural institutions do not stop atrocities or solve political dilemmas. But they can influence the way in which conflicts are imagined and interpreted. And since the interpretation of past conflicts is often at the core of new ones, that is not a negligible role.

One of the most difficult and yet most crucial problems in contemporary culture and in the resolution of conflicts is that of dealing with the memory of suffering and injustice. Must art keep alive the memory of past wrongs? Or should it, in the name of a peaceful future, urge forgetfulness. How can the victims of conflict be honoured and memorialised without implicitly demanding vengeance?

We are, rightly, haunted by images of historical obliteration, for example the children on their way to a concentration camp in a cattle truck who were so hungry that they ate the cardboard identification tags hung round their necks and so did not even survive as names. The death of one's name, the obliteration of one's culture, increases the awfulness of death itself. Oppressors in our times have increasingly understood this. They have realised that their power is not limited to the mere infliction of physical death. They can go further and inflict other levels of death, killing a culture, wiping out the set of meanings encoded in a language, destroying the memory of those who have been destroyed.

Primo Levi (1988), who survived the Nazi Lagers (concentration camps), reminds us in *The Drowned and the Saved* that the SS guards took particular pleasure in telling their victims that their experiences would not be remembered:

> However this war may end, we have won the war against you; none of you will be left to bear witness, but even if someone were to survive, the world would not believe him. There will be suspicions, discussions, research by historians, but there will be no certainties, because we will destroy the evidence together with you . . . We will be the ones to dictate the history of the Lagers.

One of the crucial roles of artists in the face of conflict is to ensure that the barbarians do not dictate history, that there can be an imaginative life after the death they inflict on their victims. But we should also be haunted by images like Jonathan Swift's Struldbruggs in *Gulliver's Travels*, who live forever but who, because 'they have no remembrance of anything but what they learned and observed in their youth and middle age' have become 'incapable of friendship and dead to all natural affection'. Historical oblivion is terrible, but so is the kind of selective remembering that makes people incapable of friendship in the present.

The problem of steering a course between the children who ate their names on the one hand and the Struldbruggs on the other is not just a problem of culture, it is a real and immediate problem of politics. The philosopher Hannah Arendt, who did her great work in the wake of Hitler and the Holocaust, reminds us, in words that have, if anything, grown in relevance, that political action is impossible without the capacity to forgive and be forgiven:

> Without being forgiven, released from the consequences of what we have done, our capacity to act would, as it were, be confined to one single deed from which we could never recover. We would remain the victims of its consequences forever, not unlike the sorcerer's apprentice who lacked the magic formula to break the spell.

That release from the consequences of what has been done is a part, too, of what cultural institutions must try to achieve. It is not, of course, easy for communities in conflict to come to terms with history, especially when each of them can, with some justice, see itself as the victim. Grief and grievance, when they are not shared but divided, give people a bleak but firm foothold on the present. The Danish philosopher Kierkegaard writes 'I say of my sorrow what an Englishman says of his house: my sorrow is my castle'. Sorrow is where, in a place shaped by violence, many people live, and it may, for some, be an impregnable castle. Art must be able to acknowledge its force while refusing to be trapped within its walls.

The balance between the kind of obsessive return to past wrongs that imprisons people in the past and the kind of willed amnesia that consigns the hard-won lessons of the past to oblivion is a difficult one. We know, because we are told so often, that those who do not remember history are condemned to repeat it. But it is just as true that those who cannot forget history are also condemned to repeat it. What artists have to do is not to forget the past or to be trapped by it but to find a way of remembering it that releases us from the belief that its consequences are inevitable and inescapable. They have to find a way of telling the story in which it remains possible to re-write the ending.

And this, perhaps, is the central task of artists and cultural institutions in a situation of conflict. To be freed from the awful Hobson's choice of either taking sides in the conflict or ignoring it, they must engage in what Kierkegaard calls 'remembering poetically':

> The more poetically one remembers, the easier one forgets; for remembering poetically is really another expression for forgetting. In a poetic memory, the experience has undergone a transformation in which it has lost all its painful aspect.

Kierkegaard talks too of a kind of forgetting which honours the grief of the past by shaping it into a tool for making a better future, a kind of forgetting that 'is the shears with which you cut away what you cannot use, doing it under the supreme direction of memory'.

What he means, I assume, is not that we should consign painful memories to mere oblivion but that we should use art to give them a shape and dignity that transforms their meaning. Whatever else it does, art must not be an instrument of evasion or denial. We know, in any case, that denial merely postpones, and perhaps deepens, the trauma of conflict and that injustices driven underground will germinate and re-emerge, sometimes with even greater force. Still less is the idea of 'poetic memory' an attempt to suggest that art compensates us for the grief of conflict, that, for example a great war painting like Picasso's *Guernica* somehow makes up for the atrocious bombing it commemorates or that the novels of Nadine Gordimer can be balanced against the terrible apartheid system that made them possible.

Nor am I suggesting that the function of art is to beautify reality by giving us noble images of what were, at the time they were committed, dirty deeds. On the contrary, great artistic images often have the power to make us look at horrific reality with a shock of recognition. James Gilligan, a psychiatrist who works with the criminally insane, reminds us of the stark contemporary reality of what we sometimes take to be entirely mythic images:

> In the worlds I work in, Oedipus is not a theory, or a 'complex'. I have seen Oedipus — a man who killed his father and then blinded himself, not on stage or in a textbook but in real life. I have seen Medea — a woman who killed her children in response to her husband's abandoning her for another woman. I have seen Othello — a man who murdered his wife and then took his own life. I have seen Samson . . . and I have seen him many times — men who have brought the roof down on their own heads as the only means of expressing their boundless rage . . .

Sophocles, Euripides, Shakespeare and the anonymous Old Testament author may have created images more noble and beautiful than life, but they help us, nonetheless, to see life itself.

What Kierkegaard was getting at, I think, is the power of art to mediate between amnesia on the one side and imprisonment in the past on the other. It is in the nature of art to change what it touches. By remembering poetically, art can, in a purely symbolic sense of course, change death into life, barbarism into creativity, obliteration into immortality. It can reverse the process of violence, restoring meaning to the victims and taking it away from the victimisers.

Such an act of creative, honourable forgetting is the end of the great Greek tragedy, *The Oresteia*, in which a cycle of death and vengeance is brought to a close by an agreement to consign the memories of past violence, represented by the Furies, to a place underground where they will be honoured and acknowledged but also rendered benign. They leave for their new role with a blessing that is worth repeating:

> May faction, sedition,
> forever flesh-hungry,
> civil disturbance,
> cycles of slaying,
> never bray in this city,

its dust never gulp
the blood of its people,
the state get ripped open
by the rages of bloodgrudge,
a chainlink of murder.

References

Arnold, M., *Culture and Anarchy* (Cambridge: Cambridge University Press, 1960 edition).

Jameson, F., *Postmodernism or the Cultural Logic of Late Capitalism*, (London: Verso, 1991).

Kiernan, B., *The Pol Pot Regime: Race, Power and Genocide in Cambodia under the Khmer Rouge 1975–9* (New Haven: Yale, 1996).

Levi, P., *The Drowned and the Saved* (London: Sphere, 1988).

Malcolm, N., *Kosovo: A Short History* (London: Macmillan, 1998).

Steiner, G., *Language and Silence* (London: Faber, 1979).

 **Brendan Kennelly**

Hart

(1)

Lead me out of myself
and I'll persuade
Knockanore Hill to run down
and dive into the Shannon,
persuade that river
to lead you and me
past the scavenged castle
and the silent island
to the sea.

Four years old —
Hart walked the road
past the garage
and the creamery
over the bridge
between the trees
by the fountain and the stream
to the National School
where three teachers waited:

> Warner
> Mulcahy
> Kiely

Warner taught him to write A,B,C
and the other letters that would grow
stranger with the years.

'Come up to the blackboard, Hart, and write
M and W for me. Make a word
With M and W in it. Take your time.'

Hart had seen it in a comic:
Old Mother Riley was his source.

MIAOW!

He chalked it on the blackboard.
Warner smiled, patted him on the head.
'You learn from cats' he said.

From Old Mother Riley, thought Hart,
from Billy Bunter and Desperate Dan,
Keyhole Kate and Inspector Stanley.

Warner said memory is the future.
Hart didn't know what to make of that
                at the time.
He does now, half a century later.

'Let the Pagan and the Christian talk
                to each other.
Put in memory what they say' Warner said.

Hart was Oisín, the pagan poet.
Patsy McKibbon was Saint Patrick.
They colloquied for weeks until
their voices lived in each other.
(Forty years later, doing his work
after a storm, McKibbon was electrocuted in West Cork).
Pagan, Christian, Christian, Pagan.
The words danced in Hart's head.
'That's what the Irish are' Warner said
to himself in a low voice. Hart heard him,
put the words in his memory.
Memory is the future.

'This is the world' Warner said,
pointing to a map on the wall.

'This is land' he said, 'and this is the sea'.

Land. Sea. Africa. America. Europe. Asia. Australia.
Hart looked at the letters of the words of the continents
of the world. Only Europe didn't start with A.

Did that make Europe different in a way
only the alphabet understood?

Why, as the letters lit his mind,
did they haunt his blood?

Atlantic Pacific Baltic Aegean Indian Ocean.
Seas words whisper say.

The Shannon was only a few fields away.
Who made the world? God. Who is God?
Continents. Seas. Bambury's field
where Bambury's bull mounted the cows of the parish
and the boys watched, enchanted.
Over the tall wall was the girl's school.
Hart never saw them watching Bambury's bull.
'What constitutes a mortal sin?' Warner asked.
'Grievous matter, perfect knowledge, full consent'
                    Hart replied
and hadn't a bull's notion what the words meant.
Memory is time's mercy on what we never understand.

Let whoever will, be king of the sea:
Bambury's bull is king of the land.

'Who is the Holy Ghost? Where is Limbo?
Name the Five Glorious Mysteries.'

        Over the fields the Angelus rang.
            People stopped their work and prayed
        in Carrig Ballyline Pooleen Lenamore
            and the Cross of the Wood.

        Memory took off its cap and whispered
            of the bits-and-pieces dead
        who'd worked the fields in their own way
            to earn their daily bread

        and nightly love. The bell faded like a song
            in a pub late at night,
        faded into the pagan dark
            and the Christian light.

'Your body is a temple of the Holy Ghost' Warner said
to the Mouse Mulvihill, 'Who could ask for more?'
The Mouse put the question
to two corner-boys, a fisherman
and a woman back from Birmingham
but the Holy Ghost had slipped out the back door.
'Say that again' Warner said. 'And again',
voice, eyes, hands commanding.
'My bub-bub-body is a Tut-tut-Temple of the Holy
            Gug-Gug-Ghost', the Mouse repeated
his skinny knees stammering.

Patsy McKibbon knew an appletree.
He gave two apples to Hart
who ate them sitting on the school wall
swinging his legs in freedom.
He gave McKibbon tuppence in return.
Two red apples, juice
like out of Bambury's bull.

Grievous. Perfect. Full.

Mortal.

What age is he now?
What age is mortal sin or the appletree
or Patsy McKibbon
making S and U
on a blackboard in eternity
that has no memory
or is nothing but memory
or is nothing dreaming of nothing?

Two red apples. Tuppence. McKibbon electrocuted.
Bambury's bull pumping like mad.
Hart is a promising lad, Warner said.
A promising lad.

(2)

Hart spent two years with Mulcahy
who should never have been a teacher.
He hated the job.
He seemed to hate the boys
and taught them only one thing:
Fear.

They'd never forget that. Never.

Monday morning. Mulcahy sat at his table,
refusing to look at them.
He read the *Irish Press* with bloodshot eyes,
smoked Woodbine cigarettes with shaky fingers,
twenty a morning, twenty an afternoon.
His fingers were brown with Woodbine smoke
and when those fingers twisted Hart's nose
the stink of Woodbine smoke
stayed in Hart's blood forever.
The priest smoked Sweet Afton.
The doctor smoked Gold Flake.
Mulcahy was a Woodbine maniac.
Woodbine stank in his words:

            'You're a crowd o' lazy curs!'
                    he shouted at the boys
        and slapped Tom Connor twenty times,
                ten on the right hand,
                ten on the left
                        because Connor couldn't name
                the Five Sorrowful Mysteries
                    or subtract
            41 from 3,239
                    or multiply
                    25 by 17
                or point out
                    Vladivostock
            on the map of the world.

        'You lazy, stupid çur' Mulcahy shouted,
                lashing Connor again and again.
        'You're not fit to sweep the dirt off the streets
                and your father was the same.
                Have you any bloody shame?'

Tom Connor hung his head,
Tears falling on his burning hands.

Time's mercy on what no-one understands.

Who said?

Tom Connor understands it all too well
Although they say he begged the streets of Liverpool
But we're not sure of that.

Bloody hell!

Winter evening, up a cold dark lane,
hidden, whispering,
Friel and McCann on Mulcahy,
the Woodbine beast:
'I'd love to crucify the bastard' Friel whispered,
'I'd love to hear him shriek with pain'.
They smoked and whispered in the darkness,
dreaming impossible revenge, the violent
teacher spurring fear and hate,
the hate and fear shaping the boys' will.
His ghost will always be too late
to ask forgiveness. Hart sees him still
in a bleak street, sweating, damning, dead.
The ghost is
what the man was.
Mulcahy has no blood to spill.
Old youngsters have real tears to shed.
Are they shed in vain?
Ask a winter evening
of outlaw smokers
up a cold, dark lane.

(3)

Better to remember a story of hurt and love
than nourish fear's deep, zigzag scars.
There are many ways to keep hate alive,
nourish it through the years.
Kiely understood a boy's fears
and could tell a story
where wonder had a place.
Hart saw pain in Kiely's face
and could never explain it
though rumours ran through the village.
Kiely was Fridays
and Fridays were stories.
He sat near a window
and let his words flow
across the room into the boys' hearts.
The words nested there, biding their time to fly.
No explanations now,
no questions, no answers,
no solutions to algebra
geometry subtraction division multiplication

      only a story

and Hart knew time could be light.
Kiely stepped from one century into another
like a farmer moving from field to field.
He shuffled images like cards,
dropped rhythms like marbles trotting round the room,
turned silent moments into pools of wonder.
Each Friday, when the story ended,
he sat, silent, in the chair near the window,
watching the boys' faces,
the pain in his own
at rest for a while.

The pain and the story were brothers
talking to each other
after a long silence.

A ghost is a story struggling to be told.

Who is chosen or compelled to tell the story?

Did any boy
ever thank Kiely?
The boys sat, listened, thought,
went away

out the door
of the National School
by the fountain and the stream
under the trees
across the bridge
past the creamery
and the garage.

After the story
Hart moved
slowly at first
then ran,
ran with abandon.

    Lead me out of myself
        and I'll persuade
Knockanore Hill to run down
and dive into the Shannon,
persuade the Shannon
to lead you and me
past the scavenged castle
        and the silent island
                    to the sea.

 **Paula Meehan**

Desire Path

For days before the kids were gathering stuff —
pallets and cast-off furniture, the innards of sheds,
the guts of Barna huts. Local factories on red alert
for raiding parties under cover of dark.

I watched them lug and drag fair-got and knocked-off
gear across the park, to the gap in the hedge,
to their deep ditched hoarding spot where they kept
it dry and guarded against the rival gang's attack.

They reminded me of bees, making to the flower
or worker ants. Their comings and goings wore

the grass away until there was only bare earth
on their preferred track — a desire path

inscribed on the sward. I reckon seen from above
it must look umbilical to some object of exotic love.

Stood Up

Leaning against the tree for over an hour,
young man waiting — for his girl, I assume.
All Souls' Day and the leaves falling dreamily.
I've seen the girl he's waiting for, a flirt,

up at the pub with the shiny gang, a short time
ago. Skulling pints. She's having a baby.
At least that's the word out there on the street.
They say it's not his. The first day of winter

is sweet and mild and gold and blue. He looks
beyond the aspen's tremulous leaf
to where small children fan the embers

of last night's bonfire. They coax a flame. It sucks
the air vigorously, then hesitates, then takes like grief
that's easier borne now than it will be to remember.

Pyrolatry

'Our wheelie bin was missing after the bin collection today.
It has No. 13 painted in white on one side.
If you happen to see it, please let us know.'
Should I tell them about the flames I saw

earlier — the green and the purple and the blue. The way
they snaked and writhed, sometimes narrow, sometimes wide,
could only have been plastic, toxic and noxious, so
strong the smell on the breeze. I had to claw

the washing in, which hung for hours in Virgo
from the drying line, which reeled and jigged
through that constellation until dark fell

and the wind dropped its poisoned cargo.
The flames veered east, then north, the kids ligged
round; then someone turned up with a drum — autumn's knell.

Stink Bomb

The smell of which still hangs about the house
despite the scented candles, the essential oils
I've burned and censered through the rooms
like a priestess in a diabolic rite.

Of course the row we had could have roused
the undead and the dead alike. It left me coiled
in a foetal crouch behind the couch, some womb
I was trying to get back to. And shite

if we didn't wake next door's dog; the Hound from Hell
Himself right on cue. You'd have to laugh. Or die
trying. Between your irrefutable logic

and my inarticulate sobs, we missed the door bell
ringing, we missed the children singing *trick*
or treat, trick or treat, the ghost afloat, the witch afly.

Mistle Thrush

The sycamore is weeping leaves of fire;
a maple stands in its own flaming lake;
shy birches isolate in yellow puddles.
You'd half expect these young trees to kick

their fallen skirts away. Bride? Bullfighter?
Dervish dancer rapt in a swirling cape?
When I went out an hour ago to muddle
through the leafdrift at my door, a flock

of mistle thrush descended — a deputation
from the wingéd world with urgent and with fatal news:
Dying is simple. You breathe in, you breathe out, you breathe in,
you breathe out and you don't breathe in again.
They acted like this was cause for celebration
— the first minor chord of my winter blues.

Sudden Rain

I'm no Buddhist: too attached to the world
of my six senses. So, in this unexpected shower,
I lift my face to its restorative tattoo
the exultation of its anvil chime on leaf.

On my tongue I taste the bitter city furled
in each raindrop; and through the sheeted fall of grief
the glittery estate doth like a garment wear
the beauty of the morning; the sweet reek of miso

leached from composting leaves. Last night's dream
of a small man who floated in the branches of an oak
harvesting mistletoe with a golden sickle

I intuit as meaning you'll be tender and never fickle
this winter, though this may be synaesthetic
nonsense; I've little left to go on, it would seem.

Malice Aforethought

Her tongue would flense the flesh from off your back.
I've never heard her utter a good word
about a neighbour or a friend in need.
Yet half the time you'd listen to spite your self,
knowing full well tomorrow it's your turn
to squirm and be lambasted on the spit,
the faggots stacked about your feet, the match

struck and held to straw and twigs. Should it catch
and take — the whole estate is lit
in the glare and glamour, while the one who burns
discovers the heft of our black craft, our art, frail shell.
Each flaming word a falling leaf — seed
nurturer and comforter that'll one day lift a bird
from the earth to its nest, a worm in its beak.

 **David Wheatley**

A Dublin Ghost

Who is the foremost poet to have published and made his career exclusively in Ireland's capital city? Dublin has never lacked for poets, but cross off Swift, Yeats, Synge, Clarke, Kavanagh, all of whom published in Britain at one point or another, and who is there left? You will not find him on the standard-issue poster of literary greats displayed in Irish pubs, you will not find him on the Irish school syllabus, and you almost certainly will not find him in Irish bookshops. He is James Clarence Mangan (1803–1849), Ireland's *poète maudit*, an opium-eating, hard-living and hard-drinking profligate to place alongside such figures as Nerval, Edgar Allen Poe and Thomas Lovell Beddoes.

Mangan wrote almost one thousand poems and, since the collapse of Thomas Moore's reputation, is recognised as the most significant Irish poet of the nineteenth century. Yet beyond a handful of anthology pieces, his work is scarcely known. Worse, for most of the one hundred and fifty years since his death, it was not properly in print. The multiplicity of variant texts in circulation made him, depending on your point of view, a bibliographer's dream or nightmare. To give one example: Thomas Kinsella's *New Oxford Book of Irish Verse* includes a two-verse poem of Mangan's called 'Shapes and Signs'. A presciently semiotic title, you might think, until you discover that Mangan in fact wrote no such poem. What he did write was the thirteen-verse 'Moreen: A Love Lament', which he presented as a translation from the Irish of the otherwise unknown Charles Boy MacQuillan. A seven-verse version of this poem was published as an original work in 1849, now entitled 'The Groans of Despair', while a later nineteenth-century printing whittled away five more verses to give 'Shapes and Signs', as reprinted by Kinsella.[1] A multi-volume and scholarly *Collected Works* begun in 1996 has helped clear up all this confusion, but the last paperback selection has been out of print for decades.

Yeats elected him to his personal pantheon in 'To Ireland in the Coming Times' ('Nor may I less be counted one / With Davis, Mangan, Ferguson') and the undergraduate James Joyce delivered a lecture on him to his fellow students. More recently, Brian Moore wrote a novel, *The Mangan Inheritance*, about a returning immigrant investigating his family connections to the poet and (to compare great things with small) I myself decided in 1998 to follow Mangan's trail around Dublin for the purposes of a sonnet

---

1   I am indebted to Chris Morash's 'Mangan: The Definitive Edition' (*Irish Literary Supplement*, vol. 18, no. 1, Spring 1999, p. 22) for these details.

sequence. In a time when few Irish writers' tracks have not been followed and signposted for the literary tourist, Mangan remains elusive. Despite spending his entire career in Dublin (he apparently left the city only once in his life, to visit neighbouring County Meath) his poetry is almost entirely devoid of topographical detail. As the MacQuillan example shows, he frequently presented original poems as translations, and in the same way his truest portraits of Dublin can be found in poems ostensibly about somewhere else entirely. Consider the exhilarating 'Siberia', written in 1845 just as Ireland was about to sink into famine:

> In Siberia's wastes
>   The Ice-wind's breath
> Woundeth like the toothèd steel.
> Lost Siberia doth reveal
>   Only blight and death.
>
> Blight and death alone.
>   No summer shines.
> Night is interblent with Day.
> In Siberia's wastes always
>   The blood blackens, the heart pines.
>
> In Siberia's wastes
>   No tears are shed,
> For they freeze within the brain.
> Nought is felt but dullest pain,
>   Pain acute, yet dead;
>
> Pain as in a dream,
>   When years go by
> Funeral-paced, yet fugitive,
> When man lives, and doth not live,
>   Doth not live — nor die. [. . .]

Mangan was born on Fishamble Street along the quays to the south of the River Liffey, originally 'Fish Shambles' after the local market. To one side loom Sam Stephenson's Civic Offices, erected amid much controversy in the 1980s after Viking remains were discovered on their Wood Quay site. Conservationists waged a long-running but fruitless campaign to stop the development, and perhaps in honour of their efforts the footpath around the offices is studded with plaques depicting axe-heads and other heritage placebos. On nearby Winetavern Street tourists can have the full Viking experience in 'Dublinia', where one thousand years of Irish history are given the audiovisual treatment in ye olde Irish speak.

'We'd rather have the iceberg than the ship, although it meant the end of travel' Elizabeth Bishop wrote, and where tourism is concerned it often seems we Irish would rather have the interpretative centre than the troublesome historical reality.

Halfway along Fishamble Street stands the George Frederick Handel Hotel, named in honour of the first performance of Handel's *Messiah* on the spot in 1742. Today, the music in the bar leans more to house and techno, though given the sampling of Bach's *Air in G* in a club hit there may be hope for Handel yet. Georgian Fishamble Street catered for less elevated pleasures too: in 1764 Darkey Kelly was publicly burned to death for keeping a notorious brothel. Only one house has survived from Mangan's time. Standing in isolation until recently, it now rubs rooflines with an apartment complex of the sort that springs up almost overnight wherever an old tenement or Georgian hulk has been obliging enough to collapse.

Mangan was not the only celebrated Dubliner to have been born here: there was also Henry Grattan (1746–1820), leader of the short-lived Irish parliament abolished in 1801, under the Act of Union, and Archbishop James Ussher (1581–1656), a Protestant divine chiefly remembered for his claim that the world had been created on 23 October 4004 BC. At the foot of the street is St Michael and St John's church, like so many inner-city churches now deconsecrated. Like other *poètes maudits*, Mangan nursed a passion for theatrical self-abnegation (calling himself 'a ruined soul in a wasted frame: the very *ideal* and perfection of moral and physical evil combined in one individual'), but unlike Baudelaire with his callow satanism, Mangan remained a devout Roman Catholic all his life. His faith would often take him to the cellar of the old Rosemary Lane chapel, where he would perform his penitential exercises prostrate on the floor.

To one side of Fishamble Street is the city's cultural quarter, Temple Bar. When journalists reach for the most dreaded cliché of all about contemporary Ireland, the Celtic Tiger, this is the place they have in mind. In the early 1980s, repertory cinema hardly existed in Ireland, Dubliner's coffee flavours of choice had yet to end in 'o' and Temple Bar was a down-at-heel collection of second-hand clothes and record shops and car parks. There was talk of turning it into a central bus station. Then something happened to the Irish economy, and today it packs in more galleries, recording studios and cybercafés than many other counties combined.

In 1798, Ireland was convulsed by the rebellion of the United Irishmen, a tragicomic footnote to which unfolded in the month of Mangan's birth. On 23 May 1803 a raid on Dublin Castle was led by the 25-year-old Robert Emmet, one of Ireland's most romanticised revolutionaries and almost certainly its most inept.

Emmet fled the scene after the murder of the Lord Chief Justice, was captured almost immediately, and hanged and beheaded outside St Catherine's Church on Thomas Street. His speech from the dock (memorably travestied in the Sirens chapter of *Ulysses*) is one of the most stirring in the annals of nationalist martyrology. 'Let no man write my epitaph', he told the courtroom: 'When my country takes its place among the nations of the world, *then*, and *not till then*, let my epitaph be written'.

From his early teens, Mangan lived across the river from Fishamble Street in Chancery Lane beside the Four Courts, one of the city's Georgian masterpieces, and like the Custom House further down the quays, the work of James Gandon. Vacant lots and defenceless old buildings make easy prey for property developers, but here and there anomalous corners of the old city persist. One such is a large Victorian redbrick structure around the corner from the Four Courts, bearing the legend 'Dublin Christian Mission'. Mangan's Dublin was the site of intense evangelical activity, throwing up colourful characters such as Charles Walmesley, author of *The General History of the Christian Church* in which he predicted that all Protestants in Ireland would be wiped out in 1825. 'Pastor Fido' responded with a rival prophecy that the Pope was the Antichrist and would be destroyed the following year. The precise theological position of the Dublin Christian Mission must go unrecorded, since in spite of numerous visits I failed to find it open for business even once. The only sign of life came when, squinting through the curtains one day, I found myself looking at two blue and yellow parrots, one chewing intently at his perch. Could there be more than phonetics to connect the parakeet and the Paraclete?

It is a long time since Dublin's northside was the centre of Georgian high society. Our new-found affluence has not had much impact on the long-term unemployment and heroin addiction that affects the north inner-city, with a criminal underworld thrown in for good measure. Attempts to make the northside fashionable have produced some garish pubs of barn-like proportions, 'themed' for maximum exoticism. Drinkers at 'Pravda' are surrounded by socialist realist kitsch and effigies of long-dead Soviet despots. Around the same time it opened, if only for symmetry, a restaurant called Mao appeared on the southside. On the city's main thoroughfare, O'Connell Street, a statue of the dying hero Cuchulainn in the General Post Office commemorates the revolutionaries of 1916. In Samuel Beckett's *Murphy*, Neary 'seized the dying hero by the thighs and began to dash his head against his buttocks, such as they are'. Today the principal indignity he faces is the embarrassing Anna Livia fountain in the centre of the street outside his window, seldom turned on and usually full of discarded burger boxes. Nelson's Pillar, once the focal point of the street, was blown up by the IRA in 1966, but is finally to be replaced by a 120m 'Twenty-first Century Light Monument'. Mercury will pulse along the spiral designs on the side, while at the top the illuminated point will sway gently in the breeze, producing Celtic 'synergy'. No piece of public statuary can be said to have entered Irish public consciousness without being christened with a derisive rhyming nickname (Anna Livia is better known as the Floozie in the Jacuzzi) and early candidates for the new monument include the Spire in the Mire, the Pin in the Bin, the Hypo from the Corpo and the Stiletto in the Ghetto.

Elsewhere on O'Connell Street, the statues form a more traditional assembly of patriots and prelates. At the southern end of the street stands Daniel O'Connell flanked by four lugubrious 'Victories', one sporting a bullet hole through the nipple. O'Connell won Catholic Emancipation in 1829 with a series of mass rallies, stopping short of the revolutionary measures advocated by the next figure down, Young Irishman William Smith O'Brien. O'Brien's abortive rising took place in 1848, earning him five years in Van Diemen's Land. Mangan was attracted to the Young Ireland movement, writing frequently for Thomas Davis's paper, *The Nation,* before moving on to the more heated pages of John Mitchel's *The United Irishman* in his last years. Mitchel too served his time in Tasmania, before escaping from Australia for the US in 1859. Here he edited Mangan's poetry, as well as serving more time in prison, this time for his vehement pro-slavery views during the Civil War (revolutionary idealism evidently had its limits).

Further along the street is Father Mathew, the 'Apostle of Temperance', whose crusade for total abstinence became a nineteenth-century mass movement to rival O'Connell's. At its height, in 1840, it claimed five million people, much to the discomfiture of the devout but bibulous Mangan. Wags claim that Father Mathew's admonishing finger is in fact pointing in the direction of Mooney's bar on nearby Abbey Street. If so, it would not be the only connection between religion and alcohol in Ireland. Until recently, all licensed premises were obliged to close for an hour between 2.30 and 3.30 p.m. in what was dubbed 'holy hour', an attempt to dissuade feckless Irish menfolk from spending the entire day in the pub. An old Dublin joke describes a man being refused a pint of stout by the barman, holy hour having just struck. Glum-faced, he turns to leave, but the barman calls him back: 'Perhaps you'd like a drink while you're waiting?'.

Several hostelries known to have been frequented by Mangan remain in business. On Camden Street there is The Bleeding Horse, with its maze of interconnected rooms, upstairs and downstairs. There is Mulligan's on Poolbeg Street, an eighteenth-century coach house within whose walls the smoke of centuries appears to have lingered, griming over everything not already grey, dark brown or black in colour. A perverse testimony to Mulligan's authenticity is the complete absence of the literary tat with which so many Irish pubs are now accessorised. Mangan and Joyce may have drunk there, but you will have to go elsewhere if you are looking for portraits of either on the wall.

Mangan's first employment was as a scrivener, that peculiarly hopeless profession shared by his fictional contemporaries Akakii Akakievich and Bartleby. He worked at Kendrick's office on York Street, only a few doors away from the Dublin residence of Charles Maturin, author of the Gothic classic *Melmoth the Wanderer*. Across from York Street, in St Stephen's Green, Mangan confronts us again, in a handsome bust by Oliver Sheppard commemorating the tow-haired young poet rather than the alcohol- and consumption-ravaged specimen he became by the end of his life. Also on the southside is Trinity College, where Mangan worked in the library in the early 1840s. Although it produced such patriots as Wolfe Tone, Robert Emmet and Thomas Davis, Trinity was (with Dublin Castle) the epicentre of unionist hegemony in Ireland. There is more than a little irony, then, in Mangan's contributing simultaneously to the *Dublin University Magazine* and *The Nation*, as he did during this time. John Mitchel has left a memorable description of the poet in the library:

> . . . an unearthly and ghostly figure, in a brown garment: the same garment, to all appearance, which lasted to the day of his death; the blanched hair was totally unkempt, the corpse-like features still as marble; a large book was in his arms, and all his soul was in the book.

His job at the college did not last, and Mangan's last years were spent in increasing destitution. These were also, however, his years of greatest artistic triumph. There are few phenomena in Irish literature to compare with the torrent of verse he produced between 1845 and 1849, including 'Siberia', 'Dark Rosaleen', 'Sarsfield', 'O'Hussey's Ode to the Maguire', 'To the Ruins of Donegal Castle', 'The Deserted Mill' and the outstanding 'A Vision of Connaught in the Thirteenth Century'. A collection of translations, *Anthologia Germanica* (1845), was the one and only book of Mangan's published during his lifetime. A second volume of translations, *The Poets and Poetry of Munster*, appeared shortly after his death from cholera-related malnutrition in June 1849. Also from his last years is the *Autobiography*, written at the request of his confessor. Like so much of his oeuvre, this had been unavailable for many years before the completion of Irish Academic Press's edition of his *Collected Works*. But even now that he is in print again, to speak of Mangan's canonisation seems less than accurate. On the contrary, it is part of Mangan's disruptive genius to place such a concept under serious strain. If order and stability (textual or otherwise) are prerequisites for admission to the Arnoldian or Eliotian canon, on both counts he remains recalcitrant and unassimilable. The textual history of his work is only the most obvious symptom of his fundamental apartness from the mainstream of Victorian verse. Readers who take the trouble to seek him out will not be entering a Celtic adjunct to Tennyson and Browning, but a strange and uncharted region like nothing else in nineteenth-century poetry.

My sonnet sequence done, I walk from Fishamble Street to the derelict and atmospheric Misery Hill on the Dublin quays, and think of the end of Mangan's 'Siberia':

> In Siberia's wastes
>   Are sands and rocks.
> Nothing blooms of green or soft,
> But the snow-peaks rise aloft
>   And the gaunt ice-blocks.
>
> And the exile there
>   Is one with those:
> They are part, and he is part,
> For the sands are in his heart,
>   And the killing snows.
>
> Therefore, in those wastes,
>   None curse the Czar.
> Each man's tongue is cloven by
> The North Blast, that heweth nigh
>   With sharp scymitar.
>
> And such doom each drees,
>   Till hunger-gnawn,
> And cold-slain, he at length sinks there,
> Yet scarce more a corpse than ere
>   His last breath was drawn.

Sonnets to James Clarence Mangan

Fishamble Street, the Civic Offices
Turning the sky a bureaucratic grey
Above a vacant lot's rent-free decay:
Craters, glass, graffiti, vomit, faeces.
One last buttressed Georgian house holds out
Precariously against the wrecker's ball
Or simply lacks the energy to fall
And rise again as one more concrete blot.
Ghost harmonics of the first *Messiah*
Echo round the Handel hotel and mix
With bells long redeveloped out of use
At Saints Michael and John's, a ghostly choir
Rising and falling until the daydream breaks . . .
Silence. Of you, Mangan, not a trace.

*

While Dublin's 'mass of animated filth'
Was being urged by Shelley to revolt,
A childhood slum, its beetles, damp and mould,
Was loosening your flimsy grip on health.
An older brother mysteriously dead,
Parents that you couldn't blame enough:
What better way to cast your home life off
Than changing into someone else instead?
Of all the masks you donned, which one was you:
'An Idler', 'Peter Puff Secundus', 'M.E.',
'Selber', Shakespeare's 'Clarence', all or none?
Your self dispersed more than it ever grew,
A dizzy paper trail, your fate to be
A nation's anonym, 'The Nameless One'.

*

A folio creaks open, coughs a decade
Of stored-up dust into your prying face.
Wrinkled, foxed, strong evidence of fleas . . .
The book itself is scarcely less decayed.
The race is on. Your poems gather speed,
Realising time is running out.
And not for you alone: leaking rot,
The barren harvests run to barren seed.
But at your College desk your books retain
Their unavailing charm, a Provost's bust
Still pledges learning's universal salve.
That can no more save the land from ruin
Than spare you that incalculable waste.
That spectacle. Your country left to starve.

*

Let the city sleep on undisturbed,
New hotels and apartment blocks replace
The Dublin that we brick by brick erase;
Let your city die without a word
Of pity, indignation, grief or blame,
The vampire crime lords fatten on its flesh
And planners zone the corpse for laundered cash,
But let your heedless cry remain the same:
'The only city that I called my own
Sank with me into everlasting shade.
I was born the year that Emmet swung
And died my fever death in forty-nine:
My words are a matchstick falling through the void
And scorch the centuries to come with song.'

A Humber Sonata

'UFF' daubed on a loyal empty lot,
our great deliverer, a stirrupless
King Billy over a spotless gents',
the city gates closed against King Charles,
the vowel sounds thinning out to only
a ferry trip away from Dutch
(these days even the fish are imported).

*

The municipal chewing gum removal operative
(who can tell birdshit from gum at fifty paces)
inches his wildly throbbing
motorised gum-remover forward,
circumnavigating Queen Victoria
for the second time, rolls
the pulpy mass of gum in his mouth,
rolls all its sweetness . . . up into one ball,
spits its out and goes on his way.

*

(*It being the habit of the beetle,*
the time it lifts its head in summer,
to sway as it goes about
and not stoop to any small flower
there might be in the field
or blossom in the garden, be they
roses or lilies, but to fooster along
until it finds a cow's leavings
or horse's mard in which to wallow.)

*

All you can drink for a fiver in a dive
I know down by the quays if you're not
doing anything better on Friday night.

*

Important announcement:

THE TWO ESQUIMAUX
OR YACKS
male and female, brought home
by Captain Parker of the Ship *Truelove*,
of Hull, from Nyatlick, in Cumberland Straits,
on the West Side of Davis' Straits
WILL BE EXHIBITED
ON THURSDAY AND FRIDAY,
MARCH 9TH AND 10TH
IN THE LECTURE-HALL, YORK
for two days only, previous to their
return to their native country on the 20th instant . . .

*

A lazy-paced sloop arcs
round the flour mill churning
the tributary a finer shade
of stirred-shit brown, waits
for the coursing Humber high tide
to wipe its arse.

*

Startling, the purposeful
back and forth
of a duck's arse-feathers
in the garden next door

like a doily being primped

while the s-bend neck
leans into the basin and drinks

glug glug

what was it she called me
finding my hair uncombed?

Dáithí Lacha, 'Davy the duck'
(meaning 'duck's arse')

*

Further important announcement:

Mr WHATEMAN
respectfully informs the inhabitants
of Beverley & its vicinity
that the wonderful
FISH
supposed to be the species of the
MERMAID
from its perfect resemblance to the
HUMAN FIGURE
which was caught a few weeks ago by
the crew of the Davis' Straits ship, Mary Frances
will be exhibited for four days only . . .

*

Schools and children half price.

**Martin Maguire and
Michael Mulreany**

'Our sedate suburb, the capital of What Is'

'Our sedate suburb, the capital of What Is': thus the Pulitzer prize-winning, American poet, John Berryman, described Ballsbridge in his collection *The Dream Songs*. Berryman spent a year in Dublin in 1966/7. He said he chose Dublin because 'it's right on the edge of Europe, it's crawling with delightful people and they all speak English'. Apart from these peripheral Anglophone delights, the poet had a gladiatorial motive: he had come to grapple with his own poetry and 'have it out' with Yeats's 'majestic shade'.

Berryman lived in Ballsbridge in 'a trim suburban villa' — 55 Lansdowne Villas — and drank nearby in 'Jack's lounge' — Jack Ryan's pub in Beggars Bush — where photographs of the poet can still be seen. Ballsbridge, originally Ball's Bridge, named after the engineer who created a bridge over the River Dodder in 1791, is indeed a sedate suburb, located roughly a mile southeast of central Dublin. The phrase 'the capital of What Is' suggests that Ballsbridge was central to Berryman's life; but of course it might also be an ironic reference to the suburb's sense of self-importance. Whatever the case, the poems in *The Dream Songs* are strewn with local references: Herbert Park, the American Embassy, Slattery's bar. Alongside contemplations about Irish saints, Berryman ponders about the man who made a pass at his wife. His balanced conclusion was that 'The country is full of con-men as well as the lovely good'. *Plus ça change.*

In a city of the literary stature of Dublin, it is natural that its centre and near suburbs should have their literary ghosts, their blue plaques. Like Berryman, Patrick Kavanagh, who lived at 62 Pembroke Road, wove a sense of place into his work. One thinks immediately of the Grand Canal and Raglan Road and of how Kavanagh charted them into the city's literary geography. The paths of the two great poets crossed briefly at a poetry reading by Berryman, but when, in his introductory remarks, Berryman thanked a man Kavanagh could not abide, the Irish poet stormed out.

What of Yeats, the 'majestic shade'? Yeats was born at 5 Sandymount Avenue, but the area laid little claim to his poetic sensibility. Though at a more prosaic level, there are local references in the Yeats family's correspondence, such as attending rugby matches at Lansdowne Road.

61 Lansdowne Road was the home of Denis Johnston the playwright, biographer and war correspondent (not to mention lawyer, actor and theatre director) and his wife the theatre director Shelah Richards. Their daughter, the novelist Jennifer Johnston,

also lived there in her youth. In the article which follows in this volume, his son, Micheal Johnston, writes about the house and the family association with it.

Due to Denis Johnston's theatrical connections, his home played a small part in the history of film in Ireland: some 'interior' scenes for the silent film *Guests of the Nation* were filmed using specially assembled sets in the back garden. Shot in 1933 and 1934, the film is notable for early screen appearances by Barry Fitzgerald, Cyril Cusack and Hilton Edwards. It is based on Frank O'Connor's eponymous short story, set during the Troubles, in which two British soldiers are held hostage by the IRA. Ironically, the Johnston family, including the then 15-year-old Denis, was held hostage on Easter Tuesday and Wednesday 1916 when four IRA men commandeered 61 Lansdowne Road as a vantage point against a British army division bound for Dublin from Dún Laoghaire.

In the book *Orders and Desecrations*, Denis Johnston recounts how the IRA men took over the top part of the house. They made holes beside the upper windows and openings in the interior walls and barricaded the stairs with broken beds and furniture, promising that any damage would be made good by the Irish Republic. The Johnstons found their captors to be polite and apologetic, and Mrs Johnston made them tea.

In the event, the British Army division did not come into sight and the IRA men evacuated peaceably in plain clothes. They left behind their slouch hats, bandoliers, leggings, rifles (only one of which was later found to work) and some deadly 'Dum-dum' bullets.

Another important literary address is 60 Shelbourne Road, one of many homes occupied by the Joyce family. It was from there on 15 June 1904 that the 22-year-old James Joyce wrote to Nora Barnacle at Finns Hotel after she had failed to show up for a rendezvous. He wrote that he had 'gone home quite dejected' and hoped to make 'an appointment . . . if you have not forgotten me'. It is commonly believed that the appointment was kept on 16 June 1904, the day on which *Ulysses* is set and which Bloomsday commemorates.

Alongside its lofty literary associations, Ballsbridge and its environs can boast a colourful history.

Amongst the Anglo-Norman invaders of Ireland who accompanied Strongbow, Earl of Pembroke in 1169, was Walter de Rideleford. de Rideleford excelled in the battle for Dublin city and, as a reward, the victorious Strongbow made him Lord of Bray and gave him grants of land. The land included the estate of Meryon, extending south of Dublin from present-day Merrion Square, along the coast as far as Blackrock and inland as far as present-day Donnybrook.

But it was with the arrival of the Fitzwilliams, who came with King John to Ireland in the early thirteenth century, that the consolidation of what was to become one of the great estates of the Dublin area began.

The Fitzwilliams became the largest lay landowners and the chief resident gentry in the south of Dublin. Their residence, Merrion Castle, destroyed during the rebellion of 1641, was opposite the railway crossing at Merrion Gates, where the residential centre for the blind now stands. The estate lands were crossed by the two main roads south out of Dublin city. The first followed the present-day Baggot Street and Merrion Road to Dalkey, then the main port for Dublin. The other followed the present-day Donnybrook Road, fording the Dodder River, into the rural south county to the monastic lands at Deansgrange.

There was little building or development on the estate. The earliest record of substantial building is from 1334 when Thomas Bagod (later Baggot) built a castle near the rath in the area where Waterloo Road meets Baggot Street.

In 1454, the city corporation ordered the expulsion from the city of 'all men and women of Irish blood'. The expelled Irish of Dublin formed a new community two miles to the east of the city within the Fitzwilliam lands in a wild coastal area of sandy marshes which came to be called Irishtown. During the reign of Queen Elizabeth I a new haven was developed at Ringsend, near Irishtown, replacing Dalkey as the main port for Dublin city.

During the early eighteenth century, the coastal area around Blackrock became a fashionable site for summer seaside residences for the gentry. The Fitzwilliams built a new house at Mount Merrion, approached by a long avenue from Blackrock, which is the present-day Merrion Avenue. One of the most imposing of these new summerhouses was Frascati House, built on the site of the present-day Roches Stores in Blackrock.

At that time, the fashionable area of Dublin was to the north of the River Liffey. In 1745 James Fitzgerald, the Earl of Kildare and, later, Duke of Leinster, chose to build a townhouse on the unfashionable southside on lands leased from the Fitzwilliams. Where the Dukes of Leinster went, fashion soon followed. Leinster House, now the site of the Irish houses of parliament, established the south of the city as the most stylish area for the gentry to live in.

From 1750, roughly one hundred years of orderly and coherent planning and development transformed the fields and meadows of the Fitzwilliam estate into magnificent Georgian squares and streets. As the development of the estate progressed, the family recorded its ancestry and its marriage alliances in the street names. Merrion Square, to the east of Leinster House, was begun in 1762. The development of Denzil Street (now Fenian

Street), Clare Street and Holles Street (called after Denzil Holles, Earl of Clare, cousin to the Fitzwilliams) began at the same time. On its western side, the estate development was co-ordinated with that of Leeson, Earl of Milltown. The immense urban space of Merrion Square established a benchmark of design and quality of workmanship for the rest of the development. Fitzwilliam Square continued the pattern and, by the time of the Act of Union of 1800, the Fitzwilliam estate was established as the most fashionable part of Dublin.

Though building continued, the era of classicism and grandeur had in fact come to an end with the Union. Almost in sympathy with the end of the Irish parliament, the Fitzwilliam family itself died out. In 1816, the Fitzwilliam estate passed to Lord Herbert, the 11th Earl of Pembroke, a family into which the Fitzwilliams had married in the late eighteenth century.

Dublin city in the nineteenth century was a city of decline and decay. The end of the Irish parliament shifted the focus of society to London. With the departure of the aristocracy, the success of the building programme on the Pembroke estate depended on the middle class. As the Georgian squares of the formerly fashionable northside were acquired by speculative landlords and subsequently decayed into slums, the middle-class professionals moved to the southside suburbs. Their street names, apart from those carrying the family titles, commemorate victories of the British armies of the early century: Wellington, Raglan, Elgin, Waterloo. The houses were no longer as grand as those of the Georgian period but were sufficiently grand to appeal exclusively to the better-off middle-class professionals. The Pembroke estate had a policy of only allowing building work that was beyond the pockets of the lower classes, thus making the area exclusive.

Lansdowne Road, built in 1855, is typical of the type. Part of it was originally called Haig's Lane after a whiskey distillery built beside the Dodder. After the distillery closed it was demolished and the rubble was used as a foundation for Lansdowne Road. There is some uncertainty about the name Lansdowne. William Petty, who took the title Marquis of Lansdowne in 1784, was married to Sophie Carteret whose country home was Lansdowne Hill in Somerset. He also had a great grandfather and namesake, William Petty, who in the 1650s originated and directed the first scientific mapping of Ireland, which was called the Downe Survey because the land was mapped directly down on paper rather than merely described. Either derivation is plausible and perhaps it was the coincidence of both that decided the choice of title.

Basically Georgian in character, the houses on Lansdowne Road are three stories over a ground floor 'basement' with a flight of granite steps to a first floor main entrance. Where the houses were built in semi-detached pairs, the front door was moved to the side. The ground floor housed the kitchen and servant quarters, the rest of the house was for the family. The lavish plasterwork of the earliest houses is replaced by simpler and more functional detailing in those built later.

With the growth of the estate as an area of middle-class residents, the demand also grew among tenants to have some representation in the administration of the estate. In 1863, despite the resistance of the Pembrokes, an Act of Parliament established the Pembroke township, comprising essentially the suburbs of Ballsbridge, Ringsend and Irishtown. It was to be administered by elected commissioners and was to provide for 'lighting, paving, sewage, draining, cleansing, supply of water and otherwise improving and regulating the township . . .'. The architect and developer Edward Henry Carson, himself an elected commissioner, designed Pembroke Town Hall, now the VEC building beside the RDS at the junction of Anglesea and Merrion Roads. Carson was the father of the more famous Edward Carson who mobilised Ulster Protestant resistance to Home Rule in 1912. Despite the presence of the commissioners, the Earl of Pembroke still maintained a paternalistic control over the township. A considerable proportion of the estate rental income was reinvested in drainage and sanitary services by the Earl, reflecting perhaps the concerns of the professional classes that dominated the tenantry. Higher standards of services, however, meant higher taxes and the Pembroke township grew to have far higher rates than the neighbouring Rathmines township.

In contrast to the great homes of the wealthy, like those on Lansdowne Road, the old, industrial, working-class areas of Rings-end and Irishtown were verminous slums. But, with a very high ratepayer franchise, the commissioners of the township acted primarily in their own interests and kept expenditure to a minimum. The working-class area of the township was ignored until 1869 when an epidemic of typhus fever swept through Ringsend and Irishtown, underlining the lack of sanitary facilities in the area. It was not until the fever swept through the exclusive residential areas of Raglan, Clyde and Elgin Roads in 1879 that action was taken: the township fearing the damage to its reputation amongst the wealthy classes. During the 1890s, artisan dwelling schemes with modern sanitary services were developed in Ringsend. By 1914, over three hundred had been built.

Around 1900, Lansdowne Road was a quiet residential quarter for the professional middle classes. At the end of the road the occasional train broke the suburban silence, stopping at the station on the railway south to Kingstown (Dún Laoghaire). From the corner of Northumberland Road to the Shelbourne Road intersection, where the Jurys and Berkeley Court hotels now stand, the Trinity College botanic gardens provided an exotic parkland.

A sense of the social composition of, and indeed family life on, Lansdowne Road in 1901 can be gained by looking at the households that lived there, for example, in the houses that today form the Institute of Public Administration. Number 49 housed the Black family, John and Ellen, 53 and 50 years of age respectively, and their unmarried daughter Rachel, aged 22. John Black was a wine merchant. The family was Protestant, Church of Ireland and were all born in Dublin. Also forming part of the household were two servant women, both Catholic: Ann Horan, a 45-year-old cook and a native of Dublin, and Teresa Culladine, a 20-year-old housemaid from County Offaly.

Number 51 was an even smaller household comprising John Pollen, 80, a widower and retired accountant of 'no religion' and two servant women: Mary Green, 28, a cook and Bridget Robinson, 20, a housemaid. As was usual, the servants were Catholic. Mary Green was born in India, probably the daughter of a soldier. Bridget Robinson was born in County Westmeath.

The two Atkinson sisters, Georgina and Sarah Maria, lived in number 57. Both were Protestant, Church of Ireland, and natives of Dublin city. Georgina at 59 was the elder sister, and Sarah Maria was 56. Both were unmarried and lived on an income derived from investments. Minding them were two servant women. Helen Mary Lee, 26, a Catholic from County Cavan was the cook. Kate Shaw was a Protestant, Church of Ireland, from Galway city; a widow aged 28, who was the parlour maid. A parlour maid was an 'upstairs' servant and a grade above a housemaid. Protestant servants were unusual so perhaps Kate Shaw was, as a widower, an 'unfortunate' case taken on as an act of charity.

Number 59 had one of the largest households, eleven persons in all, on Lansdowne Road. The Bradshaws, a Church of Ireland family, were headed by Robert, a 39- year-old land agent from County Wexford and his wife Agnes Margaret, 44, from Scotland. The children ranged from one to eleven years of age. Agnes Helena was 11, Charlotte May was 9, Marion Pearl was 5. Robert, the only son, was 2 and no doubt the heir to the family fortunes, and the youngest child was one-year-old Eleanor Margaret. In attendance to the Bradshaw family were four servants: Katherine McAteer, 28, a Catholic from Ravensdale in Cumberland in England; two sisters from Blackrock, Lucey Anne and Hannah Newman, both Church of Ireland, one 28 and the other 21 years of age. Finally, there was Elizabeth Hendrick, a 27-year-old Catholic from Cologne in Germany, a governess to the children.

In number 61 was the family of Thomas Whelan, Assistant Inspector General of the Royal Irish Constabulary and thus a man of some importance. Thomas Whelan was 62 years of age, a member of the Church of Ireland and a native of County Wicklow. His 57-year-old wife Harrietta was from County Roscommon.

Living with them was Florence, an unmarried daughter of 31 years who had been born in County Carlow. Two Catholic servants looked after them: Bridget Moore, 38, from County Laois and Frances Cassidy, 25, from County Meath.

On the eve of August 1914, in the last summer of peace, the shadows of a very different future were already encroaching on the Protestant and unionist enclave of Lansdowne Road. In fact, the township had been in trouble for some time. The exclusion of the lower middle classes such as clerks meant that there simply were not enough 'quality' tenants in rundown, provincial, late nineteenth-century Dublin.

By 1900, development in the Pembroke township had stagnated. Rates were held artificially low in an attempt to attract more development; it was supposed that the Earl could be relied upon in the event of a crisis. Matters were made worse when the township secretary absconded with the funds. The democratisation of local government in 1898 changed the Pembroke township commission into an urban district council and extended the franchise to women and the working class. By 1911, the council membership was overwhelmingly Catholic and nationalist. The Earl of Pembroke withdrew his largesse in distaste at this turn of events, thus precipitating a financial crisis. Despite these financial problems, the residents still fought to preserve the exclusiveness of the Lansdowne area. Strong objections were raised to a proposal in early 1914 to build housing off Northumberland Road for the working class. It was not until 1919 that local residents agreed to withdraw their objections and a beautifully designed scheme, the Pembroke Memorial Cottages, was built.

The Easter Rising of 1916 signalled even more revolutionary changes. The Third Battalion of the Irish Volunteers, under the command of Eamon de Valera, occupied Boland Mills. They established themselves in strategic positions along Northumberland Road as far as Mount Street Bridge. As British Army reinforcements marched into the city they were caught in a devastating crossfire and Mount Street Bridge saw the greatest number of casualties inflicted by the insurgents on the British forces. The Boland Mills garrison of 117 volunteers was the last to surrender, laying down arms on Sunday 30 April before being marched down Mount Street and Northumberland Road to imprisonment in the Pembroke Town Hall.

The area saw sporadic shooting during the War of Independence and the Civil War. The barracks at Beggars Bush, on being vacated by the British Army, became the headquarters of the Free State forces under Michael Collins.

The politics of the Pembroke township also changed. In 1918, the South County Dublin constituency, mostly the Pembroke township, elected the Sinn Féin candidate Desmond FitzGerald, father of Garret FitzGerald. But the financial problems of the township grew. Efforts continued to meet the urgent housing needs of the working class. Many of the larger houses went into decline as the middle classes moved further out into the suburbs. They were, in any case, too large for a world in which servants were no longer plentiful or cheap. Many were subdivided into apartments and flats. Some were turned into offices and the residential tradition declined. In 1930, the attempt to maintain Pembroke as an independent, self-governing township was abandoned and it was incorporated into Dublin City.

The city has prospered and changed and the suburbs of Ballsbridge, Ringsend and Irishtown have changed with it, as evidenced by rising property values and enclaves of upmarket townhouses and apartments. In 2000, the New York real estate agency, Corcorans, listed property in Ballsbridge among the twenty most expensive locations in the world!

A generation on, would John Berryman still recognise Ballsbridge as a 'sedate suburb'? Some of the long-established institutions have gone. The Irish Sweepstakes, once the largest lottery in the world, has been wound-up and Goffs Bloodstock Sales has relocated to County Kildare.

Other venerable institutions are going; University College Dublin's veterinary school, which has been located between Pembroke Road and Shelbourne Road for over one hundred years, is scheduled to relocate to more modern premises on the UCD campus at Belfield. Located among the cool software companies and the upmarket hotels, its earthy smells connect passers-by to a simpler past. Previously, the Trinity College botanic gardens vacated the sites now occupied by the Berkeley Court and Jurys hotels. University scholarship of the plant and animal kingdoms is moving on.

Other long-established institutions remain. The Royal Dublin Society (RDS) began a protracted move to Ballsbridge in 1880 when it leased 15 acres from the Pembroke estate. The Society, founded in 1731, had acquired Leinster House in 1815; its first Spring Show was held in 1831 and the Horse Show was first held in 1868 in the grounds of Leinster House. Both shows transferred to the more spacious environment of Ballsbridge in 1881 and have remained there since. In 1924, the government of the Irish Free State purchased Leinster House and the Society transferred its headquarters to Ballsbridge. The neo-classical façade of the new home of the RDS was constructed between 1924 and 1928 in a style that now seems slightly unfashionable but with detailing and workmanship that command attention.

In the same year that the RDS first leased land in Ballsbridge (1880) the Masonic Order of Ireland commenced building its school for orphans. The Masonic Female Orphan School was opened in 1882 and strove from the outset to educate girls in an environment that was 'carefully sheltered from the trials and temptations of life'. In 1973, the school was closed, sold to the RDS and renamed Thomas Prior House after a founder member of the Society. The RDS subsequently re-sold the building, which is currently Bewley's Hotel. The Masonic Order symbols of the compass and rule and the stars of David and Solomon can still be seen in the windows and stone carvings.

At the corner of Elgin Road and Pembroke Road, on the site previously occupied by Bord Fáilte, is the American Embassy. Completed in 1964, the rotunda-style building still manages to look modern, though it imitates ancient fortifications with a moat of shrubbery and entrance bridges.

Lansdowne Road is dominated by the rugby stadium — the oldest international rugby stadium in the world. Ireland first played England there in 1878. In 1880, again against England, Ireland scored its first try; but it was not converted so, according to the rules of that time, there was no score. England converted their try and won. Currently, the Lansdowne Road stadium is used for a variety of sporting fixtures, most notably international rugby and soccer matches. Plans for other stadia have been mooted but Lansdowne Road occupies a special place in Irish sporting affections, additionally so because of the ascendancy of soccer and the association of the stadium with the success of the Irish soccer team in the late 1980s and early 1990s.

At 57 to 61 and again at 49 to 51 Lansdowne Road, just across from the stadium, is the Institute of Public Administration, the Irish public sector development agency. Established in 1957, it acquired its first property on Lansdowne Road in 1960. Its founders were distinguished public servants: one of the signatories of its articles and memorandum of association, Dr Garrett FitzGerald, later became Taoiseach. They were conscious of educational models from abroad such as the Ecole Nationale d'Administration in Paris with its profound influence on the higher echelons of the French civil service and throughout French public administration. Today the IPA draws to Lansdowne Road public servants from all parts of the country as well as students from the US, central and eastern Europe and Asia

The mixing of old and new is a natural feature of progress. Market forces and urban development go hand-in-hand and intransigent conservation is as unwelcome as reckless change. Naturally the mixture has positive and negative ingredients: wealth creation and planning controversies, construction and congestion, café latte and counselling. Mercifully, this evolving mixture has maintained the essential character of Ballsbridge, which manages to elude 'gin and Jag' gentrification and remain a 'sedate suburb', except on international match days, that is.

Micheal Johnston

Etwall

I was at the first launch of the IPA Diary in 61 Lansdowne Road, at which an excellent lunch was served on the first floor in what had been, in earlier times, the upstairs drawing room of the house. I have been back annually for the Yearbook lunches since then — always a most enjoyable event which for many journalists like myself is the first engagement of the Christmas season.

But it had an added significance for me, as Etwall, number 61 Lansdowne Road, had been the house in which my father did his growing up, and was for many years the home of my grandfather William John Johnston, a County Court judge under the old regime, and judge of the High Court and eventually the Supreme Court of the Irish Free State. He was an interesting old gentleman, and from what I have gathered from various barristers who pleaded before him, well liked and well respected in his courts, even earning for himself the sobriquet Civil Bill.

I recall talking to an elderly sergeant from Irishtown garda station who remembered him very kindly, many times having passed the house late at night on his beat, and noting the light in the upstairs window where the judge was working on his judgments.

My father, Denis Johnston, was almost 15 years old when the house was occupied during the 1916 Rising, an incident he described in the preface to his play on the Rising, *The Scythe and the Sunset:*

> I was a schoolboy at the time of the Rising, and for the greater part of three days my home was occupied and fortified by four male members of de Valera's battalion, while we of the family were held, supposedly as prisoners, but actually as hostages (my father was a judge at the time). It all sounds more dramatic than it was. Our captors were soft-spoken and apologetic young men who did the least damage they could, compatible with their orders to turn the house into a fort and to prevent us from leaving. On the third day, feeling I suppose that they had by then done enough for Ireland, they stripped off their accoutrements and disappeared through the front gate, shortly before the outbreak of the major pitched battle of the week — which began at the other end of the road. I still possess a slouch hat and a bayonet that I saved from confiscation by riding off on my bicycle to a friend's house on the opposite side of the operations, with these incriminating objects concealed as far as possible in a school satchel.

Consequently my recollections of the week are personal and undramatic. Of the rebels I principally remember their charm, their civility, their doubts and their fantastic misinformation about everything that was going on. Of the men in khaki there remains an impression of many cups of tea, of conversations about everything except the business in hand, and of a military incompetence of surprising proportions, even to my schoolboy's eye.

Curiously, I remember my father recounting the story, and I thought he told me he took the loot to Rathmines on the cross tram, the rather delightful nickname used in those days for the predecessor to the number 18 bus. The reason that Etwall was chosen by the insurgents was that by knocking loopholes in the upstairs walls they could command a view of the road crossings at Ballsbridge and Shelbourne Road, and the railway.

The name of the house, Etwall, is an important part of the story of the house. I have complained at each Yearbook launch about the notable affront done to the house when the front entrance was rearranged to unite the three houses, numbers 57, 59 and 61, under the ownership of the IPA. A single entrance and a single exit were made where there had been three separate entrances before. But one of the original gateposts of my grandfather's house was moved down the road to mark the new exit at number 57. Unfortunately that particular gatepost was the one with Etwall carved into its granite facing, threatening of course to confuse scholars for generations to come. I am glad to say that at the launch in 1998 we came to an agreement that the named gatepost would be swapped over with its fellow in 2001, the centenary of my father's birth, so that the name can be properly related to the correct house in future.

Etwall, I found from a gazetteer, is a village near Derby in England, and I was curious how and when the house acquired the name. It was not a fantasy of my grandfather's — it was already on the house when he arrived there in 1915. Following the address back through the old Thom's Directories throws up some interesting information. The east end of Lansdowne Road was the last to be developed. Eastward from the Shelbourne Road crossroads was originally known as Haigh's Avenue, and where the Irish Rugby Football Union (IRFU) grounds are now was a malt manufactory, and later an athletics ground. From 1878 until 1902 the Irish Champion Athletic Club Ground occupied the site. In 1903 and 1904 it became Lansdowne Lawn Tennis Club and Wanderers Football Club. Lansdowne Football Club was added in 1905, and in 1908 it became the Irish Rugby Football Ground.

In the 1880 directory there was no 61 Lansdowne Road, but its building probably commenced that year, because it is there in the 1881 directory, described as vacant.

The next year has it occupied by a James McEnnery Esq. Cross-referencing through the directory, I find Mr McEnnery again at 18 Bridge Street Lower, trading as McEnnery Bros, wine and spirits merchants. Two other McEnnerys, Ambrose and Richard, with residences in Glenageary, are listed there with James. Possibly they were three brothers trading together, or a father and two sons — or whatever. But the name Etwall is given to the house in Lansdowne Road from James's residency there. Maybe the family came from Derbyshire?

He was only in the house for two years. The next owner was a solicitor, Robert Carey; he lived there from 1884 to 1891 — the precise years, based on Thom's, may be subject to slippage of a year in either direction, depending on the date for copy for each annual edition, and precisely when in any year moves may have happened. In 1892 the house was returned as vacant, and during that year Thomas Whelan moved in. He was the Assistant Inspector General of the Royal Irish Constabulary (RIC), working out of Dublin Castle. In 1903 and 1904 he was still there, but described as late Assistant Inspector General, having presumably attained retirement age. From 1905 to 1908 we have Cornelius Pelly Esq., JP, ex-government auditor, with his widow Mrs Pelly the householder in 1909. From 1910 to 1914 it is William H. Drennan, ISO, First Assistant Registrar of Deeds in Ireland. All of these successive owners kept the name Etwall on the house, and together they make quite an appropriate list of predecessors to the IPA — except perhaps for the wine and spirits merchant?

My grandfather was living around this latter time at 32 Elgin Road. His father had escaped from a small farm near Magherafelt and became a very successful tea-merchant in Belfast, known in the family as 'the Tayman'. He had been what is now almost a forgotten breed, a Protestant Home Ruler, and was for a time the Honorary Secretary of the Protestant Home Rule Association in Belfast. His eldest son, William, became a barrister, and obviously inherited his father's political outlook. He stood, unsuccessfully but only narrowly so, as a Liberal Home Ruler for South Derry in the second general election of 1910. When he moved into Etwall in 1915 he had been elevated to the bench, and is entered in the 1916 directory as His Honour Judge Johnston. So this became the home of my father Denis Johnston from his middle teenage years. The occupation of the house in 1916 was quite an early incident in their life there. As he grew up, the house was known for its tennis parties and other hospitality as his parents launched their only son into adult life. Rather surprisingly there are formal wedding pictures taken on the steps of Etwall on the day my parents married, 28 December 1928: I do not quite know what they were up to getting wedding pictures taken at the groom's family home.

In the early 1930s Etwall had another unusual event. My father, along with most of the young actors of Dublin, was making a film of Frank O'Connor's *Guests of the Nation*. It was a silent movie, although the talkies were already then a reality. But it was a pioneering production for Ireland. Many of the stars of the Abbey and the Gate theatres rushed around Dublin and County Wicklow taking part in the film — Hilton Edwards, Barry Fitzgerald, a very young Cyril Cusack and my mother Shelah Richards. She was married to my father then, and a number of her relations were drafted in as extras, her nephew Tony Macan who was a schoolboy kicked a football, although it was rather inappropriately an oval rugger ball instead of a round gaelic football or soccer ball; and her Aunt Georgie played the peasant woman in whose cottage the soldiers were kept captive. The interior of that cottage was a set built in the back garden of Etwall in Lansdowne Road. Occasionally in the finished film they have shot off the set, and there are little glimpses of the house and the garden walls around the edges of the pictures.

My grandparents lived in the house right up to my grandfather's death in 1940. There are photos of my sister Jennifer and myself up on the roof with my father around that time. I remember seeing those pictures as a child, and in the same set of photographs there was a younger little boy I did not know; whenever I asked who he was there was prevarication and confusion. I found out long after that it was my half-brother Jeremy, who many years later was a colleague of mine in RTÉ.

When my grandfather died, his widow Kathleen and her sister, Auntie Bell, moved to Sandymount. My father kept on the Lansdowne Road house, divided it up into flats, with his new mother-in-law Cecily Chancellor in the main first floor flat. It doubled also as pied-á-terre for himself and his new wife Betty Chancellor when they lived for periods of time in Dublin, back from London or America or wherever he was working at the time. My half-brothers Jeremy and Rory did most of their Irish growing-up there, and I certainly lived there for one holiday when my mother was ill with TB in Noel Browne's sanatorium in Newcastle. That I think would have been in the late 1940s or early 1950s. I remember Mrs Gethin lived in the flat at the top of the house, and the Maddens were in the basement/ground floor — Mr Madden owned a garage in a lane right beside my cousin's house in Adelaide Road, it was a mews lane for the houses in Leeson Street.

I do not know when my father finally sold the house — obviously after Cecily had died, and probably before he moved back to Ireland to take up residence in Dalkey — or how long may have been the interregnum between his ownership and the coming of the IPA to Lansdowne Road. My collection of Dublin directories runs out before that time. But it was the IPA's *Administration Yearbook & Diary* that brought me back to the house again in 1966. I was producing one of the daily programmes on RTÉ when the Yearbook was launched, and we featured it and its editor Jim O'Donnell on the programme. I was delighted to be asked to the launch afterwards — and it was weird to go down there and have lunch in a house I knew so well. I have enjoyed many Yearbook lunches/launches since then, although for some time it has been moved out into a building in what was the back garden — to where my father presided over those tennis parties as a young man and where Aunt Georgie made her film debut.

And now to the happy ending: in 1999 the IPA embarked on its long-promised building programme in Lansdowne Road. The IPA's Director General, John Gallagher, seized the opportunity to complete one bit of unfinished business: to see the gatepost with the name of the house, Etwall, swapped around with its anonymous brother, restoring the name to the correct house, number 61, where Mr James McEnnery, the wine and spirits merchant, ordained it should be in 1881. An institution like the IPA, dedicated to scholarship and correct procedure, wished, of course, to see this little discrepancy put right. And before the 1999 launch/lunch it had been accomplished, a year and a half ahead of schedule.

A little footnote: I showed this piece to my daughter Becky, and she said: 'But you didn't tell my story'. 'What story?' I asked. She apparently had been working in the geriatric department of St James's Hospital, and was with a long-term stroke patient, who had been unable to speak for some time. As she was by his bed he saw her nametag, and asked, quite clearly: 'Johnston? Are you anything to Denis Johnston'. She said she was his granddaughter. 'I used to deliver milk to his house in Lansdowne Road,' the man said; 'they were a lovely family and they used to have great tennis parties there.' He then lapsed back into incoherence, and nobody could believe she had had this conversation. So that is Becky's story of Lansdowne Road and my father's milkman.

The rear garden of Etwall, Lansdowne Road, Dublin, 1940

The set for an interior of Guests of the Nation, *in the garden of Etwall, 1934*

*Denis Johnston and Jennifer
Johnston on the roof of
Etwall, 1939*

*Jennifer Johnston in the garden of
Etwall, 1931*

*Micheal Johnston in the garden of
Etwall, 1939*

*Jennifer Johnston in the garden of
Etwall, 1939*

The marriage celebrations of Denis Johnston and Shelah Richards on the steps of Etwall, 1928

Tennis party in the garden of Etwall, 1920s

Kathleen Johnston with her grandchildren, Jennifer and Micheal, in the garden of Etwall, 1939

Denis Johnston with Jennifer and Micheal on the roof of Etwall, 1940

 **Frank McGuinness**

Rosa O'Doherty

d. 1660, Louvain

for Donal Gordon

I lie in Louvain, waiting for the resurrection,
A wife to a Wild Goose, a bird without wings,
Flying away from my dreams far from home.
My song is Limerick's Lament. Don't heed when I whinge.
I hear they now call it Stab City. My son
Was killed in a knife fight near here. I see the polish
Of hard steel. A stain on the floor, that's the sum
Of his life. Do you know what is my dearest wish?
To go home to Ireland and to have less patience,
To stop suffering fools. Rosa O'Doherty,
Remember my name should you forget we danced
In the graveyard of Louvain. I am ready
To forgive and fly by night since the day we sailed
To the Holy Roman empire. It lies beyond the Pale.

You should have seen the state of me upping out
Of Rathmullan. There's Donegal, my foreign fort,
Passing away from me. In my quiet way I shout,
I do not want to go. But silence is the heart's
Language. Silence is the speech of sore truth.
That I believed till the air stung my crying cheeks.
Exiles' tears are useless. Their eyes are a rath
To defend the mouth and brain from betraying ache.
I was reared a lady, virtuous, well-born.
That's what's carved on my flat tombstone. I've kept
My manners and stayed under it. Angels blow their horns
Above me, stained-glass Nativity, but women wept
In Jerusalem for the same man's lonely death.
I never shed a tear any Good Friday. Too many wreaths.

I have no time, no sympathy for my own self,
I ceased long ago to have truck with mysteries.
I have time for the wine glass, the dirty delft,
The annals of meals eaten. I have time for history
That tells me a man caught a fish, the fish spoke —
It was a wonder. Somewhere near Carndonagh,
That's where this happened. The fish was a hake.
It could tell fortunes, it could read palms, it saw
The future. The future itself looked like a dead son,
Like the sea with no ships. In Rome my husband died.
His corpse smelt of herring, fresh herring. The moon
And myself went wild. I'd hold him in my wide
Arms, hearing waves sing, You're leaving Inishowen,
Rosa O'Doherty, you'll never again see home.

Is it good to sit in the city of Louvain
Drinking water? That's all I can manage,
Remembering Ireland, remembering the pain.
My stomach is churning, this water tastes foreign
My hands have turned into cats' claws, they have the itch
To kill. I could catch a rat with my teeth.
It would taste like raspberry jam, sweet — still each
To her own. But when it's devoured, my breath
Would be sour as a widowed man dreaming
Of his dead wife. Of his own holy family.
Mine was never holy. It's just that we took wing
As Wild Geese never to return. I'd lost the keys
To my kingdom. Neither nuns nor priests honour us.
Before I noticed, we had turned into dust.

I'm blessed with an excellent constitution.
I can guzzle whatever's put in front of me.
Shellfish, lamb, the daintiest pastry — all one.
In the sight of God, who did not create the sea
Nor the mountain where the lamb thrived, nor
The fish that sing to me from the generous plate,
Their bones a sacred relic. It is far
From shell and mountain I now reside. The flat
Lands of resignation, in Flanders I abide.
My land-locked city, my Louvain, my grave —
If I squealed like a pig leaving Ireland, I hid
It all. I had to. I was the chieftain's wife.
How do I look to this alien people? Red,
Encased in passion flower, I neither smiled nor bled.

But Jesus, I long for the sleep of the just.
My eyes have not closed in this country.
In my dreams I'm not myself. I do as I must.
Were an angel to appear, my brother, sister,
I would burst my banks and roar out my name.
I am Rosa O'Doherty, on this earth born to wander,
Born near the River Crana, a woman now at home
To every dog and devil who kneels before her,
Now that she is lying in a grave in Louvain.
I sometimes wonder about going to America.
I wonder if we go home, will we be fleeced?
That's another story, another saga.
I'd love eight hours sleep and wake up at peace.

Eavan Boland

Outside History

There are outsiders, always. These stars —
these iron inklings of an Irish January,
whose light happened

thousands of years before
our pain did: they are, they have always been
outside history.

They keep their distance. Under them remains
a place where you found
you were human, and

a landscape in which you know you are mortal.
And a time to choose between them.
I have chosen:

out of myth into history I move to be
part of that ordeal
whose darkness is

only now reaching me from those fields,
those rivers, those roads clotted as
firmaments with the dead.

How slowly they die
as we kneel beside them, whisper in their ear.
And we are too late. We are always too late.

The Achill Woman

She came up the hill carrying water.
She wore a half-buttoned, wool cardigan,
a tea-towel round her waist.

She pushed the hair out of her eyes with
her free hand and put the bucket down.

The zinc-music of the handle on the rim
tuned the evening. An Easter moon rose.
In the next-door field a stream was
a fluid sunset; and then, stars.

I remember the cold rosiness of her hands.
She bent down and blew on them like broth.
And round her waist, on a white background,
in coarse, woven letters, the words 'glass cloth'.

And she was nearly finished for the day.
And I was all talk, raw from college —
weekending at a friend's cottage
with one suitcase and the set text
of the Court poets of the Silver Age.

We stayed putting down time until
the evening turned cold without warning.
She said goodnight and started down the hill.

The grass changed from lavender to black.
The trees turned back to cold outlines.
You could taste frost

but nothing now can change the way I went
indoors, chilled by the wind
and made a fire
and took down my book
and opened it and failed to comprehend

the harmonies of servitude,
the grace music gives to flattery
and language borrows from ambition —

and how I fell asleep
oblivious to

the planets clouding over in the skies,
the slow decline of the spring moon,
the songs crying out their ironies.

An Irish Childhood in England: 1951

The bickering of vowels on the buses,
the clicking thumbs and the big hips of
the navy-skirted ticket collectors with
their crooked seams brought it home to me:
Exile. Ration-book pudding.
Bowls of dripping and the fixed smile
of the school pianist playing 'Iolanthe',
'Land of Hope and Glory' and 'John Peel'.

I didn't know what to hold, to keep.
At night, filled with some malaise
of love for what I'd never known I had,
I fell asleep and let the moment pass.
The passing moment has become a night
of clipped shadows, freshly painted houses,
the garden eddying in dark and heat,
my children half-awake, half-asleep.

Airless, humid dark. Leaf-noise.
The stirrings of a garden before rain.
A hint of storm behind the risen moon.
We are what we have chosen. Did I choose to? —
in a strange city, in another country,
on nights in a North-facing bedroom,
waiting for the sleep that never did
restore me as I'd hoped to what I'd lost —

let the world I knew become the space
between the words that I had by heart
and all the other speech that always was
becoming the language of the country that
I came to in nineteen-fifty-one:
barely-gelled, a freckled six-year-old,
overdressed and sick on the plane
when all of England to an Irish child

was nothing more than what you'd lost and how:
was the teacher in the London convent who
when I produced 'I amn't' in the classroom
turned and said — 'you're not in Ireland now'.

Woman in Kitchen

Breakfast over, islanded by noise,
she watches the machines go fast and slow.
She stands among them as they shake the house.
They move. Their destination is specific.
She has nowhere definite to go:
she might be a pedestrian in traffic.

White surfaces retract. White
sideboards light the white of walls.
Cups wink white in their saucers.
The light of day bleaches as it falls
on cups and sideboards. She could use
the room to tap with if she lost her sight.

Machines jigsaw everything she knows.
And she is everywhere among their furor:
the tropic of the dryer tumbling clothes.
The round lunar window of the washer.
The kettle in the toaster is a kingfisher
swooping for trout above the river's mirror.

The wash done, the kettle boiled, the sheets
spun and clean, the dryer stops dead.
The silence is a death. It starts to bury
the room in white spaces. She turns to spread
a cloth on the board and irons sheets
in a room white and quiet as a mortuary.

The Briar Rose

Intimate as underthings
beside the matronly damasks —

the last thing
to go out at night
is the lantern-like, white insistence
of these small flowers;

their camisole glow.

Suddenly here on the front step
watching wildness break out again

it could be
the unlighted stairway,
I could be
the child I was, opening

a bedroom door
on Irish whiskey, lipstick,
an empty glass,
oyster crepe-de-Chine

and closing it without knowing why.

Julie O'Callaghan

Managing the Common Herd:
two approaches for senior management

THEORY X: People are naturally lazy.
They come late, leave early, feign illness.
When they sit at their desks
it's ten to one they're yakking to colleagues
on the subject of who qualifies as a gorgeous hunk.
They're coating their lips and nails with slop,
a magazine open to 'What your nails say about you'
or 'Ten exercises to keep your bottom in top form'
under this year's annual report.
These people need punishment;
they require stern warnings
and threats — don't be a coward,
don't be intimidated by a batting eyelash.
Stand firm: a few tears, a Mars Bar,
several glasses of cider with her pals tonight
and you'll be just the same old
rat-bag, mealy-mouthed, small-minded tyrant
you were before you docked her
fifteen minutes pay for insubordination.

Never let these con-artists get the better of you.

THEORY Z: Staff need encouragement.
Give them a little responsibility
and watch their eager faces lighting up.
Let them know their input is important.
Be democratic — allow all of them
their two cents worth of gripes.
(Don't forget this is the Dr Spock generation.)
If eight out of twelve of them
prefer green garbage cans to black ones
under their desks, be generous —
the dividends in productivity
will be reaped with compound interest.
Offer incentives, show them
it's to their *own* advantage to meet targets.
Don't talk down to your employees.
Make staff believe that they
have valid and innovative ideas
and that not only are you interested,
but that you will act upon them.

Remember, they're human too.

Pep-Talk to Poets from their Sales Manager

for Gerald Dawe

Alright, you Irish guys —
first off — I love ya — got it?
Hey — where's the blarney?
Quit looking like you were just included
in a 'Contemporary British Poetry' anthology
or something; we got books to sell!
Now, what abouta few Volkswagens in bogs
or grey streets with graffiti on the walls —
scenes like that;
you haven't been turning it out lately.
How come? I need stuff with slogans, guys.
Folksy stuff — know what I mean?
I'm doin my best but it's all lookin
a little like a yawner at this stage.
That's all, lads — keep at it.

I wanna see all a you extra-terrestrials
gravitating over here double quick, fellas.
'Take me to yer reader' — right, guys?
Now let's get serious — huh?
Here's your sales chart — up, up, up!
Kinda like a flying saucer discovering
new universes of humanoids who wanna book of poetry.
We're gonna capture new markets, aren't we,
and no more traitors writing
transvestite translations or we'll zap them
with our lazer gun — right?

Goils! Move yer feminist little butts over here.
Yer doin terrific. Lots of sarcasm
about what termites we guys are, lots of PMT,
lots of mothers acting square — magnificent!
My god, you're going great guns, ladies.
OOPS! I mean WOMEN don't I?
We want a lot of hype comin up to Christmas
so those cash registers keep singing.

Just one word of advice: see if you can
Virginia Woolf-up your images a bit
and who knows what we can do?
Sisterhood is powerful!

All miscellaneous misfits, up front please.
Lookit pals, *you* want an easy life,
I wanta easy life and we *all* want super-sales,
so why not give up this poetic individuality baloney
and get yourselves an angle, join a group.
My job is tough enough
without you weirdos
lousing it up even more!

Well-Heeled

So what's to live for?
I'm placing a Gold American Express card
on the cash desk — seven hundred and fifty dollars
down the drain
for a fantasy rhinestone pump
with spike heels.
Yesterday, it was paisley-gilded
black brocade lace-ups with a louis heel.
My analyst said, 'Indulge.'
So I'm indulging already!
I think I'd rather have an affair.
My Grecian slave sandals
would come in handy for that
or maybe my fuchsia satin court shoes —
depending on the man.

I started my girls off right.
As soon as they put a foot on terra firma
I got them little Edwardian slippers:
pink sides with a white toe and bow.
I can still see them teetering along
with frilly cotton socks and Easter bonnets.
I have those shoes up in the attic someplace.
I wonder which box they're in . . .

Nobody gives a damn about shoes anymore.
Will Sammy the Hong Kong mailman
want to seduce me in my red-rabbit-fur bedroom slippers?
Who's to appreciate — Glen, my spouse?
What a joke!
He trots off in his Gucci loafers to work
and you might as well be wearing
hiking boots under your negligee
for all he cares.
So I head for Neiman-Marcus Shoe Salon —
'the place for women who love shoes'.
If he doesn't notice my fantasy pumps
maybe he'll notice the bill next month
from American Express.

I had a pair of Maud Frizon shoes
that had cute fake watches on the ankle straps.
He kept mocking them by kneeling down in front of me
'to see what time it is'.

Did you tell that shrink of yours
about the Calvin Klein princess pumps
ya bought a year ago
and have never worn cause you say
they're too pretty to wear
or your Texan snake and pony skin
hand-tooled leather cowboy boots
that you wear to the supermarket —
did ya tell him that —
what does all this mean?
Glen always toys with the dramatic
rather than the mundane in our relationship.

It was a pair of white patent Mary Janes
that made me the way I am today.
I refused to unfasten the strap
out of its golden buckle.
I wore them to bed, to school,
to play in — I even took a bath
with them on once — they made me happy.
One morning I woke up
and they were gone.
Words cannot convey that catastrophe.

Last week I wore a sea-green
Suede-fronded ankle-boot
on my head to a party.
I went barefoot.
Maybe this is a development.

Bagels, Snow

I don't want to
do one of these
'sitting in a bookshop
during January
eating bagels
with my sister
whilst watching
the falling snow
in downtown Chicago
as the lights come on
at dusk' type of deals.
But she is drinking
an oversized cup of cocoa,
there are shelves of reassuring books
beside us, white lights decorate
the winter branches outside
and the tragedy hasn't happened yet
so I need to keep
the snow sparkling,
the cocoa steaming,
the bagels waiting
on a white plate
for as long as possible.

No Can Do

I know I'm a total party-pooper.
But there's no way
I can go to Red Lobster.
I have to stay home.
I have to rest.
I can't move.

Chip is like:
'How come you don't want
to go out anyplace?'

I'm this huge moose
with no hair,
a cheapo wig and cancer.
And I'm supposed to go
and eat a Seafood Platter?
No can do.

Autumn Foliage

Have you called the Foliage Hotline
like I asked you to, mister?
We are losing time here, people.
Those trees are getting atmospheric
as we speak.
Listen up, campers, can we have
a little more of the cooperation
and less of the attitude?
We need to place our fannies
in that Cherokee by 10 a.m. — tops.
One lousy gust at this stage
and those gorgeous maple leaves
are rotting debris.

Terence Brown

'Now and in time to be': Yeats at the Turn of the Century

George Yeats, the poet's wife, once told Richard Ellmann how Yeats always had his eye on posterity ('what's posterity ever done for us' asked, by contrast, a debater of the Act of Union in 1800). She spoke of his 'extraordinary sense of the way things would look to people later on'. And, indeed, the poem he wrote for her when he brought her as a new bride to the Norman tower in County Galway, which he had purchased shortly before their marriage, certainly suggests a man for whom the future was recurrently an imagined reality. There he hoped of the legend he had composed for a commemorative 'Stone at Thoor Ballylee' that its 'characters' would 'remain / When all is ruin once again'. He had also realised that less catastrophic futures could precede final ruination, for he knew that 'some limb of the devil' could

> Destroy the view by cutting down an ash
> That shades the road, or setting up a cottage
> Planned in a government office . . .
>   ('A Prayer for Going into my House').

Such a realistic view of futurity, of course, differs strikingly from earlier hopes for what time would bring to pass. In his young manhood the poet had conceived of the dim coming times as those in which readers would still be stirred by the knowledge that his heart had gone 'After the red-rose-bordered hem' ('To Ireland in the Coming Times') of occult Celtic mystery. Most famously, 'Easter 1916' had entered the names of the heroes of 1916 in a sacred time in which the people would be speaking their names for ever in the permanent reality of nationalism's 'Now and in time to be'. Furthermore, Yeats's and his wife's joint experiments in automatic writing and in spirit communication had given him to understand that he was living in an era of profound transition in which an antithetical age would emerge to privilege hierarchy, the heroic, the magical once again, as the levelling, rancorous spirit of democracy and scientific rationalism waned. A 'rough beast' was slouching towards Bethlehem to be born and nothing could prevent an epochal parturition. In 1925, Yeats, in visionary and prophetic mode, reckoned this process would begin in 1927 and would prepare for the 'new era' that would bring 'its stream of irrational force'. Even more disturbingly in 1937, as he contemplated in revulsion the heterogeneity of the modern city, he confessed that 'a vague hatred [came] up out of [his] own dark' and that he was 'certain that wherever in Europe there are minds strong enough to lead others the same vague hatred rises; in four or five or in less generations this hatred will have issued in violence and imposed some kind of rule of kindred'. Ludicrously, this might involve, as he speculated in 1938, 'a prolonged civil war . . . with the victory of the skilful, riding their machines as did the feudal knights their armoured horses'.

From the perspective of the twenty-first century, Yeats's prophecies of the 1920s and 1930s seem absurd enough. The western world manifestly has not eschewed democracy and materialism for a new order in which hierarchy and magic are the dominant values. Though it should be remembered that a poem like 'The Second Coming' (composed in January 1919) with its widening gyre, unhearing falcon, image of a lion body with the head of a man and its rough beast, seemed to many in the turbulent century now passed, to be powerfully prescient of the awesome fascination Fascist ideology would so soon exert. And as we come more fully to appreciate the crimes of socialism in the Soviet Union and in China as well as those of National Socialism in Germany, and to remember the crimes committed in manifold twentieth-century wars fought in the name of one or other kind of freedom, we can listen to some of Yeats's opinions of 1936 with understanding. For then he told the novelist Ethel Mannin: 'as my sense of reality deepens, and I think it does with age, my horror at the cruelty of governments grows greater . . . Communist, Fascist, nationalist, clerical, anti-clerical are all responsible according to the number of their victims'. And members of the New Age movement, its roots in the resurgence of Blakean mysticism of the 1960s, can admit to their pantheon of 'wise' men and women the poet of occult ambition who took astrology seriously and who saw deep patterns in history, invisible to the unilluminated multitude. For them at least Yeats can be allowed guru status. The revival of nationalisms in the post-communist world, with its echoes in post-revisionist Ireland, also allows some readers to acknowledge that the Yeats of 'Easter 1916' was responding to a deep, undeniable current of European feeling that in collective memory allows worship of the nation to redeem equivocal actions.

All of which is to say that Yeats's vision of the future was a limited one. Alert to some of the developments of European thought and politics in the first half of the twentieth century, he also instructs us how prophecy is less a matter of skrying the future than of critiquing the present. For Yeats's anticipation in *A Vision* of 1925 that the future would bring round on that unfashionable gyre again an antithetical lunar age, was more a register of his alienation from modernity than an inspired act of augury. It bespoke a profound distaste for the spectacle of mass society, and a frustrated rage that, despite all the hopes and dreams of his youth, Ireland had not escaped the 'filthy modern tide' that had risen in the western world since the seventeenth century. Yeats in prophetic mode in the 1920s and 1930s is a measure of how deeply the value system that had sustained his verse from the start had become manifestly archaic, anachronistic, out of key with the times. As, indeed, they remain. Yeats's esteem of heroism and nobility of caste, his regard for magnanimity as the basis of high courtesy in social intercourse, his acceptance that war can call forth human greatness, his regard for friendship as the prerogative of the spiritually elevated, seem as remote from the concerns of the majority in Europe and North America at the beginning of the twenty-first century as they did in his lifetime. And his association in the public mind in Ireland with a discredited and superseded Anglo-Irish elite has been a popular expression of what in the academy has been an assault on his reputation conducted in terms of a politically engaged deployment of post-colonial, post-modernist theory. In such theorising Yeats often appears as the representative essentialist — a proponent (for his own discredit-able class reasons) of a vision of unity of being and of national culture that is found disabling. For such a vision would seem to disallow the personal and social hybridity now valued as the basis of emancipatory politics.

What none of this takes account of, however, is the sustained popularity of Yeats's poetry both in Ireland and in the English-speaking world in general. In the millennial lists in the newspapers, in Ireland and elsewhere, Yeats figured largely when favourite poems of the twentieth century were voted on by the reading public. And it was the love poems, with their elevated ardour and erotic worship of transcendent beauty, so apparently remote from the assumptions and procedures of modern sexual relations, that kept getting the votes. As if to say that a romantic strain of feeling has survived a century of gender wars and redefinitions of sexual roles. So Yeats could safely have imagined an aged lover in the late twentieth century taking down his book and being stirred by a poem that reminded how in the long-gone past some man had 'loved the pilgrim soul' in her, 'And loved the sorrows of [her] changing face', without entering the feminist charge that women in this poem ('When You Are Old') are represented in demeaning stereotypical terms ('Soft look', 'glad grace', changeability).

It would be, however, to do less than justice to the power and vitality of Yeats's imagination to suggest that it is only as a romantic love poet that he can speak to our present condition on the cusp of a new century. Of the many aspects of his achievement that I would wish to single out in this short essay as bearing meaningfully on the current state of our world, it is the global reach of his mind and imagining that I wish to highlight. Born in an age when comparative religion was identifying parallels between world religions, Yeats from early manhood onwards was open to the possibility that wisdom could come from many parts of the globe, as it could from many eras. This made his orientalism, his classicism, his fascination with the Noh theatre and for occult learning, liberatingly eclectic in their unforced anti-imperialism. For there was a globally subversive spirit released in Yeats's assumption, in an age of empire, that truth can come from tales told by the peasantry of the west of Ireland, from the Tibetan slopes of the Himalayas, from ancient Egypt or Assyria, 'out of a medium's mouth'; as also there is in his ample demonstration in his poetry and drama that the English language, the tongue of the conqueror, can absorb such exotica without robbing them of the power to challenge conventional understandings. And this is a sense of things that is worth our attention today, when English is the language of a new imperium — that of a global capitalism — that knows no truths but those of profit.

Kevin Rafter

'Outside is America': The Lyrics of U2

It was an incredible sight. Two middle-aged politicians and a rock and roll star sharing a stage in Belfast ahead of one of the most momentous days in the turbulent history of twentieth-century Ireland.

It is probable that neither John Hume nor David Trimble had ever experienced anything like 18 May 1998 throughout their respective political careers. The concert at the Botanic Gardens on that early summer evening was aimed at adding impetus to the campaign to secure popular endorsement for the agreement on the future of Northern Ireland reached on the previous Good Friday. But old animosities fade slowly. Despite their shared objective in winning a 'yes' vote, the two leaders had not previously appeared together during the campaign. So it was ironic that many of the 2,000 teenagers in the audience were probably not eligible to vote in the referendum. That detail was inconsequential, however, to the images of unity provided for the television cameras as the man centred on stage between Hume and Trimble held their arms aloft in a gesture of defiant confidence in the future.

The lead singer with U2, Bono, introduced to the crowd 'two men who are making history'. Alongside the leaders of the two sides of the political divide in Northern Ireland, the singer from the Irish Republic represented the other element in the uneasy relationship between north and south.

U2 may have lambasted US foreign policy, campaigned against apartheid and raised awareness of the conflict in the Balkans, but they had never got so publicly involved in the northern conflict. At the same time in 1998, the cover sleeve of their song, 'Please', featured pictures of not only Trimble and Hume but also Ian Paisley and Gerry Adams. Although, as is noted below, the strongest identification of Ireland in the songs of U2 is through Northern Ireland, the overtly political nature of the cover was new territory for the band.

Along with the other members of U2 — Larry Mullen, Adam Clayton and The Edge — Bono is part of the first generation in Ireland to grow up with the conflict in the north. From 1969, violence became a feature of everyday life north of the border. Yet for the vast majority of citizens in the Irish Republic, the bombings and shootings were taking place far away. They were aware of the violence, but it was largely contained within the borders of the six counties. And so, the north, both physically and mentally, really was another place. In this context, it is indeed ironic that many of the songs of U2, with their roots in Ireland, draw their inspiration from the northern conflict.

The peace process in the 1990s may have increased the attention span for Northern Ireland affairs with the population of the Irish Republic. For U2, however, it was their travels in Europe and the US that brought an increased awareness of what was happening in the north. They went away to learn a little more about their home. Bono told one interviewer in 1982 that the band had become 'more aware of the political situation when we actually left Ireland. Growing up in Ireland we weren't even aware, it was so close, we were blind to the situation'.

Being members of a rock and roll band on the road opened up all sorts of new horizons for Bono, Adam, Larry and The Edge. In particular, in the early 1980s, they looked to the US to open up the door to success. They travelled the route taken by so many thousands of their contemporaries. Those emigrants, pushed out of an economically stagnant Ireland, were pulled towards the US, the land of opportunity.

While hardly economic migrants, U2, in common with so many Irish of their age and outlook, found refuge in America. Ireland was home, but the US provided both a surrogate place of shelter and a point of departure as they set about fulfilling their musical potential. Bono offered an explanation for this affinity at a concert in Texas in April 1987:

> Over the last hundred and more years, Irish men and women brought with them songs and stories on the boats and on the planes to the United States, and became a part of your music culture . . . More and more as I discover American music, blues music and gospel music, I see a real connection with the music I come from. And so, this is for us truly a sort of homecoming.

The scale of influence of the US on all facets of life is clearly evident from Bono's lyrics. They refer to Big Macs and Coca Cola; they mention place names, for example the song 'Hawkmoon 269' takes its title from a location in Rapid City, Dakota. This love affair with America is evident in 'Heartland', which evokes dry deserts, cool valleys, shining cities, the 'cotton-wool heat' of Mississippi and casts the country as a woman.

America inspired Bono. It offered him great challenges. Often it simply infuriated him. There was the anger at the foreign policies pursued by Ronald Regan during his two-term presidency in the 1980s. After a visit to Central America in 1986, where US money funded the weapons purchased in countries like El Salvador and Honduras, Bono wrote 'Bullet the Blue Sky' in which he dramatised 'those fighter planes . . . Across the mud huts where the children sleep'.

Despite these misgivings, Bono has had no difficulty in

acknowledging his American heroes. Included among these are the artists U2 have recorded with and who Bono has written songs for — Bob Dylan ('Love Rescue Me'); Johnny Cash ('The Wanderer'); BB King ('When Love Comes to Town'). Bono has also acknowledged a number of American icons. The singer Billie Holiday and her biography, *Lady Day*, inspired 'Angel of Harlem'. An exhibition on the civil rights leader Martin Luther King at the Chicago Peace Museum inspired both 'Pride' and 'MLK'. The spirit represented by Elvis Presley is captured on several songs, including the 1984 'Elvis Presley in America', with the nastier side of the Presley culture being on display on 'Elvis Ate America': 'Elvis ate America before America ate him'.

When *Time* placed the band on its cover, proclaiming U2 as 'Rock's Hottest Ticket', this was yet another fulfilment of the American dream. The Irish band had made it big in the US. They were on their way to the rock and roll hall of fame. The satisfaction of achieving success in the US was shared by the many thousands of Irish emigrants in America.

Not to be left out, those who remained in Ireland have also soaked up the American way of life. Indeed, U2 are members of the first genuine communication generation. They have, through television and the Internet, witnessed and experienced the Americanisation of all facets of everyday life. This Americanisation can be equated in so many ways with the commercialisation and secularisation of global value systems. The first three verses of 'Zooropa' contain a litany of advertising slogans — the new prayer lines. The lyrics of 'Numb', written by The Edge, take up this theme where everything is accessible yet so many options actually offer no genuine choice: 'Too much is not enough . . . I feel numb'.

While the US has provided the greatest sense of place within U2's lyrics, the changes in Europe after the collapse of communism in 1989 offered U2 a different landscape, which produced the *Achtung Baby* album. The "Europeanisation" of U2 is evident on 'Zoo Station', the title coming from the famous Berlin train station. The disintegration of Yugoslavia and the terrible fallout from the rise of nationalism across the Balkans resonated with the Irish band. The bloody, violent consequences of the break up of Yugoslavia inspired 'Miss Sarajevo'. Bono treated the political through the personal, writing about a beauty pageant that took place during the war, he asked whether there can be 'a time for different colours / Different names you find hard to spell'.

U2, through their music and involvements, have been among the most political musicians of recent times. Across all their albums U2 have cast their attention on causes and campaigns in different countries. Working as a volunteer in Ethiopia in 1985 gave Bono the inspiration for 'Where the Streets Have No Name'. The anti-apartheid campaign inspired 'Silver and Gold'. The thousands who were arrested by the military juntas in Central and South America, never to be seen again, produced 'Mothers of the Disappeared', which took its title from the organisation of the same name.

'Red Hill Mining Town' from *The Joshua Tree* album took a direct swipe at the economic policies of Margaret Thatcher's Conservative governments and their impact on British coal-mining communities. This politicisation is also evident in their association with Amnesty International and more recently Bono has been involved in the campaign to write-off the debt of developing countries.

In this context, it is probably not surprising that, in their relationship with Ireland, U2's principal statements in musical terms have been confined to Northern Ireland. Several songs over a number of albums address the conflict in the north. Indeed, U2 have actually written few songs directly about the rest of Ireland or their native city, Dublin. Those that they have written offer a glimpse of the path along which the band, and the Ireland they inhabit, have travelled — from the adolescent themes of the *Boy* album to the concerns over materialism on the *POP* album. A handful of songs contain reference points of sorts — place names, obvious descriptions, social issues. Yet those unfamiliar with Ireland or its capital city would be no wiser about the environs of these places that inspired the lyrics.

The courtship of Bono's parents is recorded in film-like sequences on 'Walk to the Water', with references to Summerhill and the North Wall. The lyrics here, in common with those in many of the early songs, tend to be sketchy and impressionistic. Another example is 'On Shadows and Tall Trees', which refers to the environment around the pylons that towered over Cedarwood Road in Ballymun where Bono grew up. As indicated by the editor of *Hot Press*, Niall Stokes, 'the Mrs Brown, whose washing turns up in the third verse, is in fact Mrs Byrne, Iris Hewson's best friend and near neighbour on Cedarwood Road'.

The highly atmospheric song 'Promenade' was written at a time when Bono lived in the Martello Tower in the County Wicklow town of Bray. A spiral staircase in the living room reached into the bedroom of the tower. A glass roof over the bed offered views of the night sky. This provided a canvas for Bono's lyrics, which conjured up a wonderfully uplifting love song that is really more a mood piece than a rock song proper: 'Turn me around tonight / Up through spiral staircase'.

More specific reference to Dublin is contained in 'North and South of the River', a 1995 collaboration between Bono, The Edge and Christy Moore. The lyrics deal with the social division of the city — north and south of the river: 'Can we stop playing these old tattoos? . . . I want to meet you where you are'.

A number of songs treat the economic and social realities of life in some of the most deprived communities in Dublin. The heroin epidemic that hit the Irish capital in the 1980s features on songs like 'Wire' and 'Bad' from the *Unforgettable Fire* album and 'Running to Stand Still' from *The Joshua Tree*. Heroin addiction drives the raw restlessness of 'Bad', while the impressionistic lyric of 'Wire' deals with ambivalence to drugs. The line from 'Running to Stand Still': 'I see seven towers', is a reference to the seven, local authority, high-rise complexes built in Ballymun in the 1960s.

However, it was the place of which they knew so little that most often brought Ireland into the songs of U2. The manner in which the band has tackled the north diverges from the traditional vein of Irish music, much of which stems from a nationalist/ republican perspective. U2 have never taken sides. In his lyrics, Bono has succeeded in exploring the conflict without being partisan.

In 1996, Bono and Adam Clayton, along with traditional Irish musician Donal Lunny, re-recorded to chilling effect an earlier U2 song, 'Tomorrow'. The lyrics have been given different interpretations including the description of an IRA attack on an isolated Protestant farm along the border between Northern Ireland and the Irish Republic. With no success, a mother pleads to her son not to go outside to check on movements: 'Outside, somebody's outside . . . Don't go to the door'.

One of the rare U2 songs penned by The Edge, 'Van Diemen's Land', is dedicated to the Fenian poet, John Boyle O'Reilly. He was deported to Tasmania for his role in organising a rebellion against British rule in Ireland. However, the song's lyrics are contemporary, dealing with the futility of violence as the scarlet coats of the Fenians give way to the black berets of the modern IRA and 'Still the gunman rules and widows pay'.

The two Bloody Sundays of Irish history, in 1921 and 1972, provide the backdrop to the most well known of the songs U2 have written about the north. Receiving the details of what happened in Dublin and Derry on the two separate days, Bono sings: 'I can't believe the news today . . .'. It may not be a rebel song, but the lyrics constitute an emotional cry of bewilderment over the loss of so many lives in the northern conflict. The anthem-style song featured first on the *War* album and later on the live mini-album, *Under a Blood Red Sky*. However, it was on the live version of the song on the *Rattle and Hum* video that full justice was done to the raw musical complement to Bono's lyrics. News of the IRA attack on a memorial service in Enniskillen, which left thirteen people dead and many more maimed and injured, had come through to Denver where U2 were playing a sell-out concert to 34,000 fans. The performance of 'Sunday Bloody Sunday' allowed Bono to join in the condemnation of the attack:

Let me tell you something. I've had enough of Irish-Americans who haven't been back in their country in 20 or

30 years who come up to me and talk about the resistance, the revolution back home . . . and the glory of the revolution and the glory of dying for the revolution. Fuck the revolution. They don't talk about the glory of killing for the revolution. What's the glory in taking a man from his bed and gunning him down in front of his wife and children? Where's the glory in that? Where's the glory in bombing a Remembrance Day parade of old age pensioners, their medals taken out and polished up for the day? Where's the glory in that, to leave them dying or crippled for life or dead under the rubble of the revolution that the majority of the people in my country don't want. No more.

While the IRA's actions in the name of Ireland never had anything more than the support of a minority of the population, Bono's passionate outburst broke from the normal complacency that three decades of violence had generated amongst the Irish public.

The terror that was visited on Omagh in August 1998 was a vivid reminder that peace is not achieved easily. Bono wrote about the bombing, carried out by the self-styled "Real IRA", in 'Peace on Earth' from the 2000 album, *All That You Can't Leave Behind*: 'Sean and Julia, Gareth, Ann and Breda / Their lives are bigger, than any big idea'.

Despite the horror of Omagh, the Good Friday Agreement does offer an opportunity for more normalised relations between the different traditions on the island. Therefore, other lyrics written by Bono can now be considered in the context of a new complacency. The increasing affluence generated by the exceptionally strong performance of the Republic's economy raises issues about the type of society that is being shaped for future generations. In this regard, lessons can be taken from songs like 'Even Better Than the Real Thing', which attempt to explain the "me-culture", the sense of having everything today without consideration or regard for the future. The dangers of importing the worst excesses of the US into the Republic are available for consideration in recent songs. All this new wealth, coupled with rampant materialism and increasing secularisation to the detriment of spirituality, could lead to the creation of a society where: 'the banks they're like cathedrals / I guess casinos took their place' ('The Playboy Mansion'); and 'the cartoon network turns into the news' ('If God Will Send His Angels').

The religious imagery, which permeates so many of their songs, offers another route for understanding U2 and the society from which they come. Yet just like Ireland, U2, both collectively and individually, have constantly sought out new influences and sources of stimulation. The songs crafted by U2 indicate a band that has gone through a process of almost permanent re-invention.

When Bono took the hands of David Trimble and John Hume, the three men could well have stopped to recollect that any normalisation of life in Ireland would bring new challenges north and south of the border. As the recent economic success of the Irish Republic creeps across the border into the north, 'Bullet the Blue Sky' may well contain an intimation of the pitfalls ahead — 'Outside is America'.

Notes on Contributors

EAVAN BOLAND is Professor of English and Director of the Creative Writing Programme at Stanford University. Her *Collected Poems* appeared in 1996 and *The Lost Land* was published in 1998. With Mark Strand, she has co-edited *The Making of a Poem: a Norton Anthology of Poetic Forms*.

TERENCE BROWN is Professor of Anglo-Irish Literature at Trinity College Dublin and a Fellow of the College. He is the author of many books of literary criticism and historical scholarship, including *Ireland: A Social and Cultural History* (1985), *Ireland's Literature: Selected Essays* (1988) and *The Life of W. B. Yeats: A Critical Biography* (1999).

GERALD DAWE is a lecturer in English and Director of the Oscar Wilde Centre for Irish Writing at Trinity College Dublin. He is the author of five collections of poetry including *Heart of Hearts* (1995) and *The Morning Train* (1999). He has also published *Stray Dogs and Dark Horses: Selected Essays* (2000).

BRIAN FARRELL is an emeritus Professor of Politics at University College Dublin, where he taught for many years. He has published extensively on Irish government and politics. He served as the first director-general of the Institute of European Affairs in Dublin and has been chairperson of the IPA's Parliamentary Internship Programme since its inception. He also pursued a parallel career as the major current affairs presenter on RTÉ, Ireland's national television service.

MICHAEL HARTNETT published some dozen books of poetry in English, including *Anatomy of a Cliché* (1968), *A Farewell to English* (1978), *A Necklace of Wrens* (1987), *Poems to Younger Women* (1988) and *Killing of Dreams* (1992). *Selected and New Poems* was published in 1994. He also published translations from Irish, Spanish and Chinese. He was a member of Aosdána, and a recipient of the American Ireland Fund Literary Award in 1990. He died in 1999. His *Collected Poems* will be published by Gallery Press in 2001.

MICHAEL D. HIGGINS is a Labour TD representing Galway West. He was first elected to the Dáil in 1981 and was chairman of The Labour Party from 1978 to 1987. From 1993 to 1997 he was Minister for Arts, Culture and the Gaeltacht. He has published two collections of poems, *The Betrayal* (1990) and *The Season of Fire*

(1993), and contributed to many political and philosophical journals.

MICHEAL JOHNSTON was one of the original television producers with Telefis Éireann at its inception in 1961. He worked for RTÉ television and radio as producer, director, presenter and reporter. He was, at various times, editor of *7 Days*, assistant controller of RTE1 and assistant head of features and current affairs for RTÉ Radio. He is author of *The Big Pot: The Story of the Irish Senior Rowing Championships 1912–1991*, published in 1992.

BRENDAN KENNELLY is Professor of Modern Literature at Trinity College Dublin. His books of poetry include *My Dark Fathers* (1964), *The Voices* (1973), *Cromwell* (1983), *Moloney Up and At it* (1984), *The Book of Judas* (1991), *Poetry My Arse* (1995), *The Man Made of Rain* (1998) and *Glimpses* (2001). *A Time for Voices: Selected Poems 1960–1990* was published in 1990. His dramatisations include *Antigone* (1986) and *The Trojan Women* (1993).

THOMAS KINSELLA is a poet whose distinctions include Poetry Society Book Choice, Guggenheim Fellowships and the Denis Devlin Memorial Award. His *Collected Poems: 1956–1994* was published in 1996 and most recently *Littlebody* and *Citizen of the World* were published in the Peppercannister Poems series (2000). He is also well known for his translations of Irish literature, including *The Táin* (1969) and *An Duanaire: Poems of the Dispossessed* (1981) with Seán O Tuama.

AODÁN MAC PÓILIN is Director of Ultacht Trust, a cross-community Irish language agency, and is a member of the North/South Language Body. He is a former Irish language editor of *Krino*. He lives in Belfast in the only urban Gaeltacht in Ireland.

FRANK McGUINNESS is a playwright and poet. He lectures in English at University College Dublin. His plays include *The Factory Girls, Observe the Sons of Ulster Marching Towards the Somme, Carthaginians, Someone Who'll Watch Over Me* and *Dolly West's Kitchen*. He has published two collections of poetry, *Booterstown* (1994) and *The Sea with No Ships* (1999). He is a member of Aosdána.

MARTIN MAGUIRE has lectured in History at the National University of Ireland, Maynooth and the IPA. He currently lectures in History at Dundalk Institute of Technology. He has contributed articles on Irish Protestant and working class identity to historical journals and is author of *Servants to the Public* (1998).

PAULA MEEHAN is a poet among whose books are *The Man Who Was Marked by Winter* (1991), *Pillow Talk* (1994), *Mysteries of the Home*

(1996) and *Dharmakaya* (2000). Her awards include the Butler Award from the Irish-American Cultural Institute and the Martin Toonder Award for Literature (1995). Her plays include *Mrs Sweeney* and *Cell*. She is a member of Aosdána.

MICHAEL MULREANY is Director of Post-Graduate Studies and Parliamentary Internship Programmes at the IPA. He is a member of Cultures of Ireland and has authored and edited texts on public management, economic affairs and European integration.

NUALA NÍ DHOMHNAILL is the author of several volumes of poetry including *Féar Suaithinseach* (1984), *Pharaoh's Daughter* (1990), *Feis* (1991), *The Astrakhan Cloak*, with translations by Paul Muldoon (1992), and *the Water Horse,* with translations by Medbh McGuckian and Eileán Ni Chuilleanáin (1999). She is a member of Aosdána and the recipient of the 1988 O'Shaughnessy Award for Poetry and the 1991 American Ireland Fund Literary Award.

DAVID NORRIS is a Senator representing the University of Dublin. He was first elected Senator in 1987. He is an internationally recognised Joyce scholar and was formerly a lecturer in Trinity College Dublin.

DENIS O'BRIEN is Assistant Registrar at the Institute of Public Administration. He teaches Irish literature at the IPA and the Gaiety School of Acting. He has previously published poems in *The Irish Times, Poetry Ireland Review* and the *British Haiku Journal* among others.

JULIE O'CALLAGHAN is a poet whose first collection, *Edible Anecdotes* (1983), was a Poetry Book Society Recommendation. Her other books include *What's What?* (1991) — a Poetry Book Society Choice, and *Two Barks* (1998) — a collection of children's poetry. Her most recent collection, *No Can Do* (2000), is also a Poetry Book Society Recommendation.

FINTAN O'TOOLE is a journalist with *The Irish Times*. He has also been drama critic of the *New York Daily News*. Among his books are *Tom Murphy: The Politics of Magic* (1987), *Traitor's Kiss: Life of Richard Brinsley Sheridan* (1998) and *The Irish Times Book of the Century* (1999).

EVE PATTEN is a lecturer in the School of English at Trinity College Dublin. She specialises in nineteenth and twentieth-century British and Irish literature and has published several articles on modern and contemporary Irish fiction. She is an editor of the forthcoming *Glossary of Irish Cultural Studies* to be published by Edward Arnold.

KEVIN RAFTER is Editor of *Magill*, Ireland's leading current affairs monthly magazine. He has previously worked as a political correspondent with *The Sunday Times*, a political reporter with *The Irish Times* and as a presenter of the RTÉ current affairs radio programme, *This Week*. The author of three books on Irish politics, including a study of Clann na Poblachta.

DAVID WHEATLEY, a lecturer at the University of Hull, was awarded the Rooney Prize for Irish Literature for his first collection, *Thirst* (1997). His second collection, *Misery Hill*, appeared in 2000. His other publications include *Stream and Gliding Sun: A Wicklow Anthology* and *I Am The Crocus*, a volume of children's poetry. He is founder editor of *Metre*.

Acknowledgements

The editors and publishers would like to acknowledge the following for permission to reprint some of the material included in The Ogham Stone.

Bloodaxe Books for Julie O'Callaghan, *What's What* (1991) and *No Can Do* (2000).

Carcanet Press for Thomas Kinsella, *Collected Poems 1956–1994* (1996) and *The Dual Tradition: An Essay on Poetry and Politics in Ireland* (1995). Eavan Boland, *Collected Poems* (1995). Paula Meehan, *Dharmakaya* (2000).

Gallery Press for Michael Harnett, *Collected Poems* (2001). Gerald Dawe, *The Morning Train* (1999). David Wheatley, *Misery Hill* (2000). Frank McGuinness, *The Sea With No Ships* (1999). Nuala Ní Dhomhnaill, *The Water Horse* (2000).